Gavin Ambrose
Harris

D0077904

PRINT & FINISH

Second Edition

Fairchild Books
An imprint of Bloomsbury Publishing Plc

50 Bedford Square
London
WC1B 3DP
UK

1385 Broadway
New York
NY 10018
USA

www.bloomsbury.com

Bloomsbury is a registered trade mark of Bloomsbury Publishing Plc

First edition published 2006
This second edition published 2014

© Bloomsbury Publishing Plc, 2014

British Library Cataloguing-in-Publication Data
A catalogue record for this book is available from the British Library.

ISBN: PB: 978-2-940496-53-2
ePDF: 978-2-940496-74-7

Library of Congress Cataloging-in-Publication Data
Library of Congress Cataloging in Publication Control Number: 2013035956

Typeset by Gavin Ambrose
Printed and bound in China

Client: The End
Design: Samuel Muir
Technical overview: Contrast of tactile greyboard cover stock, with high reflectivity, blue foil-block illustration

The End

This is the cover of a brochure that was designed by Samuel Muir for The End, a London nightclub. The End Biography celebrates the club's tenth anniversary and features commentary from music journalists, specially commissioned artist illustrations and a supplementary photo section. The cover features an illustration of the club's entrance by Will Barras, which is foil-blocked in blue into a greyboard stock. The fine line artwork reproduces well in the foil and provides a dramatic contrast with the raw quality of the greyboard.

Gloss art

C M Y K

Contents

Thomas Manss & Company

SEA Design

Lost in Lace

Studio Thomson

Studio KA

Four Letter Word

Studio Myerscough

Contents

Gloss art

C M Y K

Graphic designers have an array of print processes and finishing techniques at their disposal with which to produce eye-catching and effective publications. Printing is the process of putting ink on to a substrate, but the method a designer chooses to use to do this will depend on practical factors such as cost, volume and time, in addition to more aesthetic factors such as the quality of the visual result required. Different print processes such as letterpress, offset lithography and screen printing allow a designer to mix these variables to obtain different results, but that does not have to be the end of the printing process. Most printed products can be enhanced by some kind of finishing technique once the ink is on the paper, such as folding, die cutting, foil blocking or tipping-in coloured plates.

Substrates

Substrates come in many different weights, colours and textures and can have a dramatic impact on the end result of the job, adding texture or some other quality. This section looks at the advantages and restrictions certain stocks offer.

Printing

Different techniques for applying ink on to a substrate, such as offset lithography, screen printing, gravure and letterpress, can be used to produce creative effects, which derive from the characteristics of the processes themselves.

Finishing

Various processes can be used to provide the final touches to a print job, including die cutting, embossing, debossing, foil blocking and varnishing, which can transform an ordinary looking piece into something much more special.

Production

The physical production processes can be harnessed by the designer to produce creative results, perhaps by manipulating channels and plates or changing the order in which the process colours print so that you control the processes rather than letting them control your work.

Binding

Different binding methods such as Canadian, French folding, case and perfect, give a designer a range of different functionalities and visual qualities, which can add a special touch to a publication.

Resolve

Many printed items incorporate a range of the techniques that are discussed in this book. Interesting printing, foiling, finishing and material choices are found on the examples showcased in this section.

Drag and Drop (opposite)

Creasence made creative use of a simple die-cut for this DJ invite – referencing the spindle-hole of a 12" record.

Client: Drag and Drop
Design: Creasence
Technical overview:
Simplo but imaginative
use of a die-cut

DRAG AND DROP

21:00 / Café Sklenick
Kounicova 23, Brno
facebook.com/draganddrop
DJ Chepuchov (live)
Brezhnev
Sasha Nevolin

10.03

10.03
21:00 / Café Sklenick
Kounicova 23, Brno
facebook.com/draganddrop

DJ Chepuchov (live)
Brezhnev
Sasha Nevolin

Gloss art

Client: Zenith Interiors
Design: Frost*
Technical overview:
Die-cut aperture forming part
of a brand identity

Chapter 1
Substrates

A substrate is any stock or material that receives a printed image, ranging from a standard sheet of paper to more elaborate and tactile papers and boards, and even extends to promotional items such as coffee mugs, t-shirts and, the human body.

The substrate selected for a particular print job will be determined by its ability to 'take' a printed design and the overall aims and intention of the piece of work, as the examples in this section will illustrate. For instance, excellent image reproduction in colour magazines requires a different substrate than that used for newspapers, where low cost is more of a priority. In addition to printability, substrates are often selected for the other qualities that they can lend a design such as a tactile stimulus.

Substrate selection is a vital consideration at the start of the design process. The variety of substrates to print upon is now greater than ever before, giving wider creative possibilities for designers; as colour, weights and textures all have a bearing on the effectiveness of a piece. Identity design schemes, for example, can be strengthened through consistent use of stocks, which generates an element of individuality.

Substrates

Gloss art

Zenith Interiors (opposite)

Frost*'s identity for contemporary furniture manufacturer Zenith makes creative use of a die-cut. The strong lines of the identity create a strong architectural statement.

K
Y
M
C

Paper types
'Paper types' refers to any stock or substrate that can be printed with one of the conventional printing processes.

Paper type	Notes	Primary uses
Newsprint	Paper made primarily of mechanically ground wood pulp, shorter lifespan than other papers, cheap to produce, least expensive paper that can withstand normal printing processes.	Newspapers, comics.
Antique	Roughest finish offered on offset paper.	To add texture to publications such as annual reports.
Uncoated woodfree	Largest printing and writing paper category by capacity that includes almost all office and offset grades used for general commercial printing.	Office paper (printer and photocopy paper, stationery).
Mechanical	Produced using wood pulp, contains acidic linings. Suitable for short-term uses as it will 'yellow' and colours will fade.	Newspapers, directories.
Art board	Uncoated board.	Cover stock.
Art	A high-quality paper with a clay filler to give a good printing surface, especially for halftones where definition and detail are important. Has high brightness and gloss.	Colour printing, magazines.
Cast coated	Coated paper with a high-gloss finish obtained while the wet coated paper is pressed or cast against a polished, hot, metal drum.	High-quality colour printing
Chromo	A waterproof coating on a single side intended for good embossing and varnishing performance.	Labels, wrappings, and covers.
Cartridge	A thick white paper particularly used for pencil and ink drawings.	To add texture to publications such as annual reports.
Greyboard	Lined or unlined board made from waste paper.	Packaging material.

Client: Country Casuals
Design: Turnbull Grey
Technical overview:
Flock substrate used to
add tactile quality

Country Casuals

This invitation to a fashion preview show was created by Turnbull Grey design studio for clothing manufacturer Country Casuals. The use of a tactile flock substrate works as a visual simile to a piece of cloth, and reinforces the nature of the event that is being publicized.

Paper types | Unusual substrates

Flock

A speciality cover stock that is produced by coating a sheet with size, either entirely or partially, and then applying a dyed flock powder, which is made from very fine woollen refuse or vegetable fibre dust, to the substrate. Flock was originally intended to simulate tapestry and Italian velvet brocade. Nowadays, it is used to give a decorative, delicate and luxurious feel to designs. Flock fibres tend to be absorbent and therefore do not provide a good printing surface for conventional offset lithography, but more viscous inks can be used without any problem. The relatively robust nature of a flocked substrate means it can be used with both embossing and foil-blocking.

Gloss art

CMYK

Client: Squire and Partners
Design: Thomas Manss & Company
Technical overview: Particle-board substrate and finishing touches to reflect architecture

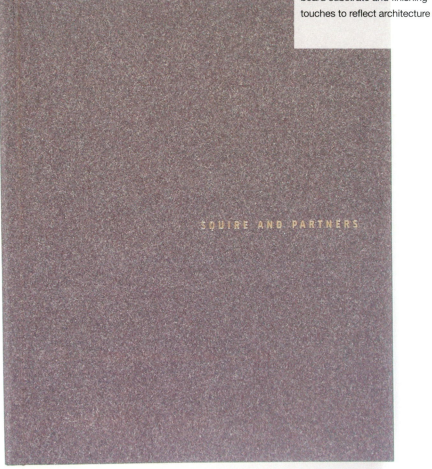

SQUIRE AND PARTNERS

Squire and Partners

This corporate brochure for London architectural firm Squire and Partners was created by Thomas Manss & Company. Rather than presenting the work in a typical corporate document, which inevitably has a limited shelf life, the designers opted for a more lavish presentation of the firm's architectural designs and projects.
The particle-board cover carries a simple foil stamp, reflecting the firm's trademark clean, modern lines and attention to detail. The cover has a monolithic appearance, reminiscent a block of carved stone, adding a degree of permanence and quality.

Client: d-raw
Design: MadeThought
Technical overview: Silver-foil
stamp into greyboard for
minimalist effect

Paper types | Unusual substrates

Gloss art

K
Y
M
C

d-raw Associates

This business card was created for interior designers d-raw Associates by MadeThought design studio. It features silver-foil type that has been stamped into light coloured greyboard, which results in a minimalist, subtle, tone-on-tone effect. The coarse fibres of the stock contrast with the accuracy afforded by the foil-stamp process.

Client: RIBA
Design: Studio Myerscough
Technical overview:
Translucent stock printing
magenta and black

Annie Spink Award Brochure

This is a brochure for the Annie Spink Award for Excellence in Education, which is awarded by the Royal Institute of British Architects. The brochure was created by Studio Myerscough and is printed in magenta and black on a translucent stock, and the text is reproduced as a surprint. The overall impact is subtle, refined and inviting. The brochure also features French fold pages with stitch-sewn binding.

Client: University of the
Arts, London

Design: Turnbull Grey

Technical overview:
Translucent cover and
duplicated design creates
moiré effect

UNIVERSITY OF THE ARTS
LONDON

Inauguration Ceremony
Banqueting House
Whitehall
London

11 May 2004

Paper types | Unusual substrates

University of the Arts, London

This is the programme for an inauguration ceremony for the University of the
Arts, London, which was created by Turnbull Grey design studio. The programme's
cover is printed on to a translucent substrate that allows the reader to see the paper
stock underneath. The paper stock carries the same design as the cover, but is
reproduced in blue with white lettering. The combination of the two produces a
moiré effect on the typography.

Gloss art

K
Y
M
C

Unusual substrates

Virtually any material can be used as a substrate to receive a design, although each presents its own application challenges.

Substrate	Uses	Application process
Metal	Signage, objects or report covers.	Screen print, transfer, hand-painted/drawn, die cut.
Ceramic	Objects.	Ceramic, hand-painted/drawn.
PVC	Signage, report covers or objects.	Screen print, die cut, transfer.
Fabric	Clothing, banners or report covers.	Screen print, hand-painted/drawn.
Wood	Signage or objects.	Burnt, screen print, hand-painted/drawn.

Her House
This invitation, created for Her House gallery by Studio Myerscough, is silk-screen printed on to a wood substrate. The slab-serif typeface has a solid quality, which allows it to work effectively with the rough wood grain surface.

Client: Zaha Hadid

Design: Thomas Manss & Company

Technical overview: Moulded plastic outer catches light, protects and lends tactility

Paper types | **Unusual substrates** | Showthrough

Zaha Hadid

This book sleeve was created for architectural firm Zaha Hadid by Thomas Manss & Company. Its moulded plastic outer creates a simple, yet intriguing statement due to the way it catches the light, and this adds value to the design. The transparent plastic also serves to provide both a protective layer and a tactile element to the high impact design and lends it a modernist simplicity.

Gloss art

8005

C M Y K

The new fab
inspired coll
from GF Smit

Client: GF Smith
Design: SEA Design
Technical overview:
Board substrate with
embossed broderie
anglaise pattern, and
bronze foil-stamped text

Tapes

London
GFSmith
2 Leathermarket
Weston Street
London SE1 3ET

Telephone
0 7407 6174
acsimile
7403 1037

n@gfsmit

Diesel (right)

This invitation was created for fashion label Diesel by George & Vera design studio. The design is screen printed on to transparent, blue-toned perspex, which results in the production of a distinctive and unusual object and is more substantial than it would have been had a paper stock been used. The use of perspex turns a disposable invite into something altogether more permanent.

Tapestry (left)

This announcement card was created by SEA Design to promote the 'Tapestry' range of fabric-inspired paper stocks produced by paper merchant GF Smith. The piece was produced on the 'Cotton White' substrate from the range, and is embossed with a digitized broderie anglaise pattern. Text was applied as a bronze foil stamp that still allows the floral pattern in the substrate to show through.

Client: Diesel
Design: George & Vera
Technical overview:
Perspex substrate is distinctive and permanent

launch

art

therese stowell

DIESEL
FOR SUCCESSFUL LIVING

Diesel P
Diesel D

Artwork
Therse

Henri M
The C.
Kensing
SW7 E

Thursd
Septem
8.30pm

Invite o
RSVP
diesel@

Florence
www.
florencefineart.
com

Laurent-Perrier
CHAMPAGNE

Armadale

Client: Patrick Heide
Contemporary Art
Design: Thomas Manss
& Company
Technical overview:
Mirror board catalogue

Light Flow – Hans Kotter

This brochure for contemporary German artist, Hans Kotter, uses a mirror board cover to reflect the nature of the artist's light-based illustrations. Rather than simply showing a piece of the artist's work on the cover, the catalogue moves away from convention and instead makes a direct visual link to Kotter's 'Colour Codes', a series of chrome boxes with a colourful back-illuminated stripe, as shown opposite.

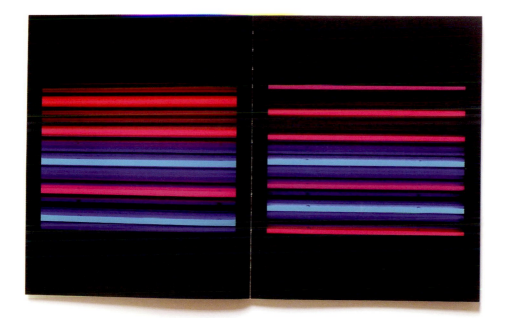

Showthrough

Showthrough occurs when ink printed on one side of a page can be seen on the other (non-printed) side; showthrough is usually determined by the type of substrate used.

Thin and absorbent stocks, with little filler or coating material, are most susceptible to showthrough. Some stocks have such a degree of transparency that subsequent pages will also showthrough. Showthrough is generally viewed as a defect, although it can be used deliberately and creatively to great effect.

Memo (above and opposite)

This is a periodical produced for architecture firm Magyar Marsoni. It features a transparent vellum insert that covers the opening image. The delicate nature of the vellum adds a tactile dimension to the publication, while allowing the opening image to show through the introductory text.

Client: Magyar Marsoni
Design: Untitled
Technical overview: Vellum insert adds tactile dimension and allows the image to showthrough

Welcome to issue one of MEMO, a new periodical from Magyar Marsoni Architects. There is a ready supply of publications about architecture and of people ready to make their views known about it. Our intention with MEMO is not so much to publish or make news as to generate a less heated, more reflective discussion of current issues in architecture as they affect a practice that is, in size at least, representative of the majority in the UK. MEMO gets its name from its loose, informal nature. The text is, literally, a discussion: the sort of ad hoc, after hours dialogue that provides both solace and inspiration to us in the midst of running an architectural practice. Each conversation, each edition of MEMO, will centre loosely on a theme. The first theme is, appropriately enough, ORIGINS.

MEMO
ORIGINS

Welcome to issue one of MEMO, a new periodical from Magyar Marsoni Architects. There is a ready supply of publications about architecture and of people ready to make their views known about it. Our intention with MEMO is not so much to publish or make news as to generate a less heated, more reflective discussion of current issues in architecture as they affect a practice that is, in size at least, representative of the majority in the UK. MEMO gets its name from its loose, informal nature. The text is, literally, a discussion: the sort of ad hoc, after hours dialogue that provides both solace and inspiration to us in the midst of running an architectural practice. Each conversation, each edition of MEMO, will centre loosely on a theme. The first theme is, appropriately enough, ORIGINS.

MEMO

Unusual substrates | **Showthrough** | Imposition

Gloss art

C M Y K

Client: Vicki and Kent Logan
Design: Aufuldish & Warinner
Technical overview: Semi-transparent stocks are used to obscure well-known paintings

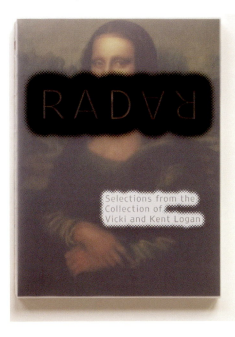

RADAR

This exhibition catalogue features selections from the collection of Vicki and Kent Logan. Semi-transparant stocks are used to obscure parts of the images, creating a sense of reveal. The cover features Yasumasa Morimura's *Monna Lisa in Its Origin (detail)*, 1998, and the semi-transparant stock, slightly obscuring the detail of the image, makes the viewer question whether it is the original or not.

Client: Boot

Design: Untitled

Technical overview:
Lightweight Bible paper
provides showthrough and
image and text interaction

Chris Boot Ltd

This is a catalogue created by Untitled for Chris Boot Ltd, a contemporary
photography book publisher. The publication incorporates a lightweight Bible
paper that enables both the production of a thin book and a small amount of
showthrough between pages. Images merge seamlessly with text, creating a
light, textured feel.

Unusual substrates | **Showthrough** | Imposition

Gloss art

C M Y K 8005

Imposition

Imposition is the arrangement of a printed publication's pages, in the sequence and position they will appear when printed; before being cut, folded and trimmed.

An imposition plan provides a visual guide with which a designer can easily see, for example, the colour fall in a section or the arrangement of different stock choices as the imposition plan shown opposite demonstrates.

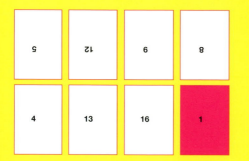

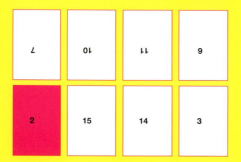

This book is printed in 16-page sections, with a single eight-page section at the end of the book.

The imposition plan opposite shows the 12 sections that go to make up this book. Sections 2, 7 and 8 print with a special colour, be it a metallic or a fluorescent Other sections print with gloss, matt or woodfree stocks, and sections 3, 4 and 10 print on coloured stocks.

The flatplan (left) shows the page fall on a sheet of paper. The sheet of paper will be printed on both sides and then folded and cut to produce a 16-page section. As each side of the sheet prints on a different pass, a different special colour can be used on either side. However, the application of a special colour will only be available to those eight pages that are on the same side of the paper sheet, either pages 1, 4, 5, 8, 9, 12, 13 and 16 or pages 2, 3, 6, 7, 10, 11, 14 and 15. When folded, pages 1 and 2 (highlighted) back up.

An imposition plan serves several functions. As well as allowing the designer to easily see where different colours and stocks fall, it can also show how they can be used to maximum effect. This one shows the stocks and colours used in this book.

1	2	3	4	5	6	7	8	9	10	11	12	13	14	15	16

Stock: Gloss art
Prints: CMYK

17	18	19	20	21	22	23	24	25	26	27	28	29	30	31	32

Stock: Gloss art
Prints: CMYK + Pantone 8005

33	34	35	36	37	38	39	40	41	42	43	44	45	46	47	48

Stock: Grey-coloured stock
Prints: CMYK

49	50	51	52	53	54	55	56	57	58	59	60	61	62	63	64

Stock: Aqua-coloured stock
Prints: CMYK

65	66	67	68	69	70	71	72	73	74	75	76	77	78	79	80

Stock: Woodfree, uncoated stock
Prints: CMYK

81	82	83	84	85	86	87	88	89	90	91	92	93	94	95	96

Stock: Matt art
Prints: CMYK

97	98	99	100	101	102	103	104	105	106	107	108	109	110	111	112

Stock: Gloss art
Prints: CMYK + Pantone 877

113	114	115	116	117	118	119	120	121	122	123	124	125	126	127	128

Stock: Matt art
Prints: CMYK + Pantone 807

129	130	131	132	133	134	135	136	137	138	139	140	141	142	143	144

Stock: Gloss art
Prints: CMYK

145	146	147	148	149	150	151	152	153	154	155	156	157	158	159	160

Stock: Green-coloured stock
Prints: CMYK

161	162	163	164	165	166	167	168	169	170	171	172	173	174	175	176

Stock: Matt art
Prints: CMYK

177	178	179	180	181	182	183	184

Stock: Gloss art
Prints: CMYK

Showthrough | **Imposition** | Tipping-in and tipping-on

Gloss art

K Y M C
CMYK

Tate Galleries

This is the members' handbook for the UK's Tate Galleries created by NB Studio. It features colour sections that are printed on high-gloss white stock, which is spliced between sections of uncoated coloured stock. This results in a contrast between the tactile quality of the coloured stock with the high reflectivity of the laminated, white stock.

Foreword
Welcome to Tate

Thank you for becoming a Tate Member. We value your support enormously and hope you will enjoy this closer association with Tate as you take full advantage of the benefits of membership.

Whether you visit frequently or occasionally, Members are part of Tate and play a vital role in our success. Your enthusiasm helps us to draw in and inspire new visitors, and creates energy throughout the galleries. You share our belief in the ability of art to change lives, and are invaluable advocates. The financial support you provide enables us to purchase and preserve works of art for the Collection, and to bring the visual arts to increasingly diverse audiences through Tate's innovative series of exhibitions, events and education programmes.

Museums and galleries have enormous potential to liberate the imagination; open doors to the past and reflect the creative energy of the present; with your help we hope to realise this potential. Thank you for supporting us today and playing your part in shaping the Tate of the future.

Nicholas Serota
Director

Client: Tate Galleries
Design: NB Studio
Technical overview: Creative imposition of high-gloss, white stock spliced between coloured stock

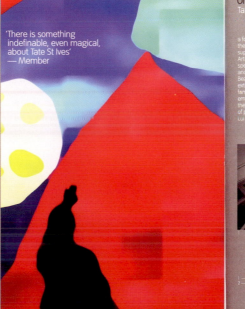

'There is something indefinable, even magical, about Tate St Ives'
— Member

One Tate, four galleries
Tate St Ives

Tate St Ives opened in 1993 to provide a focus for the St Ives School of artists within the British modern movement, while today also supporting contemporary art through the Artist in Residence scheme. The gallery has a spectacular coastal setting, with large windows and balconies offering views across Porthmeor Beach and the opportunity to appreciate the extraordinary quality of light for which St Ives is famous. Exhibitions of work by established and emerging artists are presented throughout the year, alongside changing Collection displays of painting and sculpture by artists with a connection to St Ives.

1 — View of the gallery
2 — Collection display

22 — 23

Tipping-in and tipping-on

A tip-in refers to the attachment of a single page into a printed publication by wrapping it around the central fold of a section and gluing along the binding edge.

If a tipped-in page is shorter than the publication's pages then it needs to be aligned at either their top or bottom edge. Tipping-in to the central slither can prove problematic as there is no page edge to align it with. Fine-art prints are sometimes printed intaglio and tipped-in. Tipping-in should not be confused with inserts, which are loose, unattached items that are placed inside a publication.

Tipped-in page with short return

Tipped-in page, aligned top

Tipped-in page full-width

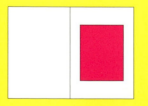

Tipping-on

Tipping-on involves pasting a smaller element, such as an illustration or reply slip on to a publication. This can create a delicate and sensitive presentation of artwork and artefacts, as can be seen in the example on the facing page.

Client: Gagosian Gallery
Design: Bruce Mau Design
Technical overview:
Tipped-on colour plates

Duplexing | Tipping-in and tipping-on | ... | Gloss art

Gagosian Gallery

This is *Six Paints and a Sculpture*, a book that celebrates the work of Cy Twombly. It was created by Bruce Mau Design for the Gagosian Gallery in New York. The book features tipped-on colour plates. Each of the plates was produced separately, and then applied to the book.

Intaglio

A technique that describes the printing of an image from a recessed design that is incised or etched into the surface of a plate. The ink lies recessed below the surface of the plate and transfers to the stock under pressure and stands in relief on the stock.

C M Y K

Client: Autograph ABP
Design: Untitled
Technical overview:
Gloss, colour pages tipped-in
to black stock

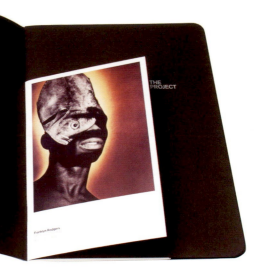

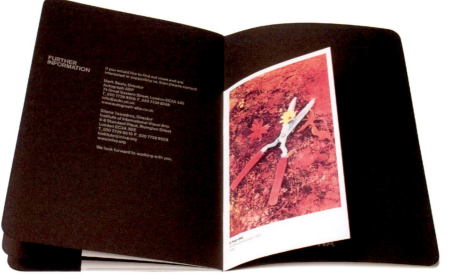

Client: Prestel
Design: Thomas Manss & Company
Technical overview: Tipped-on photograph on cloth cover

Ben Johnson, Foster in View (above)

This book is a collection of Ben Johnson's photographs of the work of acclaimed architect Norman Foster. The photographs form a reference for Johnson's neo-realistic paintings. The cloth covered edition has a tipped-on photograph, creating a personal and intimate expression of care and detail.

A Sense of Place (left)

This is a brochure created by Untitled design studio for the 'Sense of Place' project at international photographic arts agency Autograph ABP. The brochure features black pages that are printed with silver type. Gloss, colour pages have been tipped-in to the brochure and this provides a contrast of both stocks and levels of reflectivity.

Imposition | **Tipping-in and tipping-on** | Duplexing

Grey-coloured stock

K Y M C

Duplexing

Duplexing refers to the bonding of two substrates to form a single one. This allows a stock to have different colours, textures and finishes on each side.

Duplexing also increases the weight of a stock. Two duplexed 270gsm boards would produce a 540gsm substrate, for example.

Front

A virgin, venturing into a red light district

Paper from GF Smith

Reverse

Paper from GF Smith
the new collection

GF Smith would like
to invite you to an evening
of drinks, canapés and a
talk by SEA and John Ross

27 January 2005
6.30—9pm
The Fruitmarket Gallery
45 Market Street
Edinburgh EH1 1DF

Edinburgh

Front

Duplexing
Bespoke and Window Envelopes
C6/DL Envelopes
Embossing
Cut Sizes
25 Sheet Minimum Orders
Dummy Service
Sample and Advisory Services

Duplexing

Part of GF Smith
Factory Services

Reverse

Paper from GF Smith

GF Smith (above and opposite)

These invitations were created by SEA Design for paper manufacturer GF Smith and use duplexed substrates. The invitation shown on the opposite page is nubuck-brown stock with a silk-weave emboss that is bonded to an orange leatherette embossed board. Pictured above (top) is a pristine white stock duplexed to a fuchsia pink board and (bottom) a lavender stock duplexed to a candy-pink one.

Client: GF Smith
Design: SEA Design
Technical overview:
Duplexed substrates used
as invitations and product
announcements

collection
papers and
cased in an
watch will
to take away
hibition stand
and L27.

Metallic, pearlescent, tissue, iridescent, felt marked, corrugated, bible paper, onionskin, parchment, press board, archival, embossed, translucent, coloured tissue, glassine, surface enhanced papers, boards & envelopes.

Fair

Tipping-in and tipping-on | **Duplexing** | Printing

C M Y K   Grey-coloured stock

Industry view: SEA Design

Pictured are launch materials for a new range of papers by Robert Horne called *Fabriano*. Featuring iconic images by photographer Lee Funnell, each paper type is represented by a different insect.

Your work often celebrates the various qualities of stocks and printing techniques. Can you elaborate on this?

How we start a project directly affects how it is produced and finished – there is no point having a wonderful idea if it gets poorly produced on paper. There are more opportunities to express the tactile qualities within a digital age and our identity work always takes these opportunities. For example, the finish of the packaging board, the choice of texture and weight all convey emotional triggers that are lost on screen or any other medium.

Can you elaborate on the collaborative relationship between designer, client and printer?

How we produce a campaign and, more specifically, how it is printed, is all about working closely with the last person involved! We work very closely with all our printers in an almost obsessive way... Obsessing over every detail of production which I'm sure annoys some of them! However we are lucky in having some extremely passionate clients such as Monotype and Fedrigoni paper, both have produced some amazing printed productions.

SEA Design is a multidisciplinary studio working for clients in the arts, cultural and corporate sectors. They have become famous for reinterpreting how branding and identity are approached and have a clear graphic identity.
www.seadesign.co.uk

Can print and finish techniques add value and create a point of difference – difficult to create in any other way?
It's almost impossible to produce the effects in print in any other medium as print involves touch. The production process and the finished product is all about the the 'perfect' finish...

The campaign to promote the Italian paper brand within the UK was a perfect paper project. Fabriano chose a smooth white, metallic, translucent and coloured range from their vast library as a micro collection. Using hyper real images, photographed by Lee Funnell, different techniques were utilized: for example Indigo on coloured stock, a metallic "touch plate" and my favourite - reworking one of Lee's images (feather) as line art to reproduce a clear gloss foil...no image reproduced will justify this printed specimen.

Each of the paper types has distinct qualities, including texture and varying levels of transparency.

Duplexing / Industry view: SEA Design

Grey-coloured stock

C M Y K

Client: Kiwi & Pom
Design: Morse Studio
Technical overview:
Letterpress and thermography
onto triplexed card

Chapter 2
Printing

Printing is a collective term that refers to the various different techniques used to apply ink to a substrate or stock. These include: offset lithography, screen printing, gravure (or intaglio), letterpress, hot-metal, lino-cut, thermography, ink-jet and laser printing among others. Each method has its own variables such as printing speed, the available range of colours or printing capacity, in addition to cost. Different printing methods will produce different finishes on the stock. For example, a black-and-white laser printer can produce a flyer to a legible standard, but it does not leave type indentation in the stock, which would occur with letterpress printing.

The printing process is often overlooked when a job is being designed for print, but the designer should take into account the printing process to ensure that the visual impact is optimized and to effectively manage schedule and budgetary constraints.

This section highlights a number of projects that have been creatively enhanced by the wide range of effects that different printing processes can supply.

Kiwi & Pom (opposite)

Morse Studio's identity for interior and product design company, Kiwi & Pom makes use of the tactile nature of thermography (discussed on pages 54–55). The stock that it is applied to has also been triplexed – a process of sandwiching one stock between another, which reflects the design concerns and detailing of the client.

Printing

C M Y K   Grey-coloured stock

Lithography
The lithographic printing process uses a treated metal plate to transfer (offset) a design via a rubber blanket to the stock.

Offset lithography is a high-volume and speedy process that produces consistently clean results. Sheet-fed, offset litho presses are typically four-colour. Offset web litho presses use a continuous roll of paper, which allows an even higher printing volume.

Halftones

A series of screens containing halftone dots are used to replicate the continuous photographic tones in the print process. Once printed, these dots give the illusion of a full-colour image. If the screen angles of each colour were the same, interference is created and this results in muddled colours or a moire effect. For this reason each colour's screen is offset, or angled, differently. Each colour that will print is screened to produce its own series of halftone dots that will be used to make the printing plate for that colour.

Dot gain

Dot gain describes the enlarging of ink dots on the printing stock and is something that occurs naturally as the ink is absorbed into the stock. As a consequence, dot gain is more pronounced with a more absorbent paper such as newsprint. Coated stocks contain a fine clay coating which has low ink absorbency and so results in clear, sharp image reproduction.

Screen ruling

The line illustrations and photographs shown below are presented with three common screen ruling values: 60 (coarse), 133 (general purpose) and 175 (high-quality printing, like this book). Lower values give a more open screen with less detail, but this may be preferable depending upon the stock being used for printing. When printing on uncoated stocks that are more absorbent, such as the woodfree section in this book (pages 65–80), lower-value screens are used so that dot gain does not result in a saturated looking image.

60 lpi

133 lpi

175 lpi

Different images contain different amounts of a particular colour. In the example left, the red chair will be made predominantly of magenta and yellow.

Shown above are the four separated plates of the four colour image above.

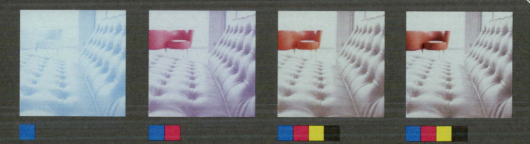

As the image prints, in this case in the CMYK order, the depth of the colours slowly builds, with the final shadows and depth being added by the final black printing plate.

Grey-coloured stock

C M Y K

Wash printing

Wash printing is a special technique that allows the most delicate of colours to be applied to a substrate.

Wash printing uses ink that has been heavily diluted in order to produce a flat colour that is more subtle than light special colours such as pastels. This wash is applied by pre-printing the sheets with a flood-colour of the diluted ink.

If this colour was applied as part of the four-colour process, it would print with a halftone dot, as shown below. Wash printing allows a subtle, sophisticated approach to colour application.

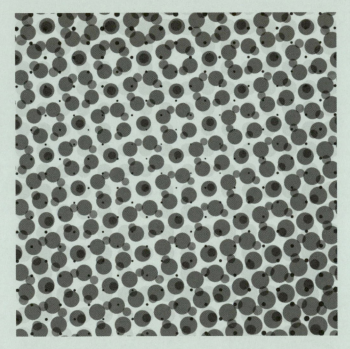

Unless printed as a special, flat area of colour, the printed finish will have on closer inspection a halftone dot pattern of the four process colours, as shown in the illustration to the left.

Brick-work (opposite)

Brick-work was created by Cartlidge Levene design studio for Sergison Bates architects. The publication features grey tipped-in pages. This subtle, flat grey is produced using a wash print with a watered-down ink to give a fine, light base colour. The first printing pass supplies this solid base colour, and then the stock follows a second, standard pass.

Client: Sergison Bates
Design: Cartlidge Levene
Technical overview:
Wash print to give light base
colour to tipped-in sections

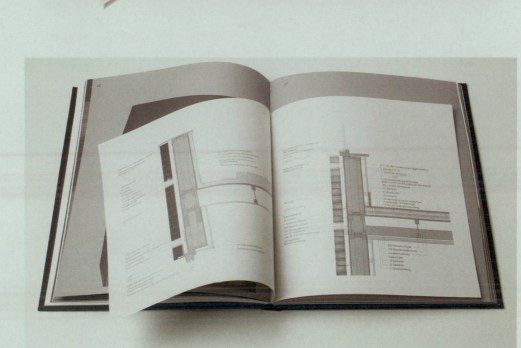

Grey-coloured stock · C M Y K · Lithography | **Wash printing** | Silk-screen printing

Silk-screen printing
Silk-screen printing imposes an image on to a substrate by forcing ink through a screen that contains the design.

Screen printing is not a high-volume printing method because each colour that is applied to the substrate has to dry before another can be applied, but it is a flexible method which can be used to apply a design to virtually any substrate. Silk-screen printing allows more viscous inks to be used, which can provide additional tactile qualities to a piece of work.

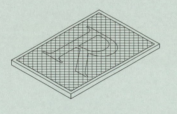

The pattern to be reproduced is fixed to a screen in such a way that ink can pass through the screen's mesh in those areas that are to be printed. The screen frame is placed over the substrate.

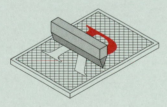

A squeegee is used to draw the printing ink over the screen, pressing it through the design and on to the substrate.

The screen is carefully removed to reveal the design that has been applied to the substrate.

Housing Services (opposite)

This folder for the University of the Arts, London, was created by Turnbull Grey design studio. The greyboard folder has been silk-screen printed in three colours (red, yellow and white). The tactile, natural feel of the greyboard is augmented by the solid and intense colours, which also enhance the tactile qualities of the piece.

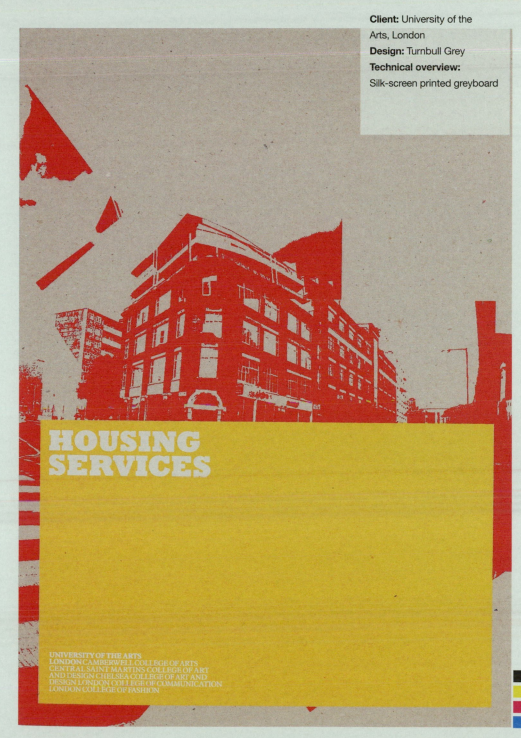

Client: University of the Arts, London

Design: Turnbull Grey

Technical overview: Silk-screen printed greyboard

HOUSING SERVICES

UNIVERSITY OF THE ARTS
LONDON CAMBERWELL COLLEGE OF ARTS
CENTRAL SAINT MARTINS COLLEGE OF ART
AND DESIGN CHELSEA COLLEGE OF ART AND
DESIGN LONDON COLLEGE OF COMMUNICATION
LONDON COLLEGE OF FASHION

Wash printing | **Silk-screen printing** | Letterpress printing

Grey-coloured stock

C M Y K

Letterpress printing

Letterpress is a method of relief printing whereby an inked, raised surface is pressed against the substrate.

Letterpress was the first form of commercial printing, and much print-specific terminology derives from it. The raised surface that makes the impression is typically made from pieces of type, but photo-engraved plates can also be used. Letterpress printing can often be identified by the slight indentation made into the substrate.

A defect of letterpress printing is that the impression from the raised surface varies every time it is pressed against a substrate, giving the characters a uniqueness where each is subtly different, which is appealing to designers. This defect has become a popular style, to the extent that an original design is printed letterpress, and the result is scanned and reproduced in offset lithography to produce multiple copies of it.

A selection of letterpress characters made from wood.

These letterpress characters demonstrate the sort of natural defects that occur on each printed impression.

Client: Pallet
Design: Studio Kluif
Technical overview:
Letterpress typography adds
character and unique identity

Silk-screen printing | **Letterpress printing** | Hot-metal printing

Aqua-coloured stock

C M Y K

Pallet

Studio Kluif's playful identity for a furniture company makes creative use of the characterful nature of letterpress typography. Because of their imperfections, the bold letterforms are personable and friendly, with a strong sense of identity.

We must always remind ourselves this: philosophy is an art form, a literary genre like poetry and fiction. The philosopher moves his concepts around on the page, just like the novelist manipulates his characters, he's certainly not producing science. But everything indicates that it is an art form in deplorable decline.

In a 21st century obsessed with utility, philosophy seems to be permanently confined to the dusty corridors of academia, where a handful of pale nerds spend their days tirelessly twisting and turning technicalities inherited from Hegel or Kant. And nobody in the outside world cares one iota. From a creative point of view, the art of philosophy seems dead.

But academia is hardly the right place to look for literary creativity; philosophy is actually doing just fine under various guises in the most surprising places. Remember that whenever we step outside the confines of our regular world view and start to question ourselves and our habitual perceptions of things, we instantly start doing philosophy. We establish a meta level, we think about thinking in a language about language.

Consequently, philosophy can, properly understood, capture the attention of a huge audience. It just isn't marketed very well at present. That could change quickly, however. We just need to remove three major misconceptions.

1. Philosophy is not an academic discipline. To take a professor of philosophy for a philosopher proper would be like regarding a professor of literature as a novelist or poet. Only rarely do these two separate functions coincide. This means, of course, that most of the relevant philosophy today is produced outside university departments, where they rather do the history of philosophy in the form of endless commentary.

A practical rule of thumb is: if a book has footnotes in it, it is anything but philosophy. It is an academic text, not art. Proper philosophy should have no more footnotes in it than fiction or poetry (Elliot is the exception that confirms this rule).

2. Philosophy is not science. Scientific rules simply do not apply. Philosophy proves nothing, and the utility value is zero, as is the case with poetry and fiction. In fact, the whole idea that human actions should be valued according to the amount of utility they produce, is itself a philosophical idea, called utilitarianism, in desperate need of philosophical scrutiny.

3. Philosophy is going big! Not in the sense of becoming omnipotent and dictating in detail how people should live their lives and build their societies. That would just amount to old-fashioned political ideology.

But big rather in the same sense that Big Science is big: aiming for a grand theory of everything. Which in the case of philosophy means a grand theory uniting the individual and collective subjects. And let's not forget that whatever Big Science comes up with, it will need Big Philosophy to work out and define the new and expanded world view that would have to accommodate a scientific theory of everything.

The philosophy of the last century, from Nietzsche via Wittgenstein to the postmodernists of the 1980s and 1990s, should be viewed as one big deconstruction project, an endeavour to expose the weaknesses and contradictions of the rationalist paradigm and the remaining legacy of the Enlightenment. But now we've reached the end of the line. There is nothing more to deconstruct, and we must not be too timid to start reconstructing. So philosophy is now beginning to move in a different direction, redefining what it means to be human, or even trans-human, in a world of interactive communication and virtual communities.

This new development should actually come as no surprise. The whole deconstructionist rage of the last century makes perfect sense when you think if it as a big house-cleaning the day before the party guests arrive. With all the shortcomings of rationalism removed, philosophy is back in good shape, ready for new adventures. And as always in the history of philosophy, the new direction is one that nobody would have expected, least of all the discarded and gloomy postmodernists themselves. The new generation of superstar thinkers – like Slavoj Zizek, Brian Massumi, Simon Critchley, and The Scandinavians – take their cues from newscasts, movie scripts and quantum physics rather than from the annals of old philosophy.

Every major transformation of information technology has, given time for absorption, caused a revolution of the mind. The reason why the ancient Greeks were able to establish philosophy as a discourse was certainly not some sort of outstanding intelligence, but simply that the organisation of society – mainly determined by the dominant mode of communication – created the first social class in history with sufficient time and means to reflect on human existence in debate and in writing. So the Greeks took what had been imported from Egypt, Babylonia and Persia, and created a new art form. Philosophy had arrived.

The next revolution occurred in Europe in the 17th and 18th centuries. The invention of the printing press had changed the feudal society completely and gave birth to a whole new class, the urban bourgeoisie, and a new demand for information and social critique. The result was the shock to the system of thought since then referred to as the Enlightenment.

And now, with the arrival of interactive information technology, the framework for social power structures and thought patterns change drastically. While the mass media obsess over the all-new gadgets, philosophy is interested in the social and cultural implications of interactivity. Nothing could be more important, since the revolution in technology inevitably will bring about a crisis of traditional values, politics, social institutions, etc. It's already happening, and it's called globalisation.

Economic and financial globalisation must be followed by a globalisation of culture and politics, since the concept of a national culture is becoming increasingly irrelevant and national politics increasingly impotent. This is the impulse for the art of philosophy to leave the deconstructionist phase behind, to start making sense of all the rapid changes, to speculate on the shape of the global political order and to give it some credibility. Add to this the ongoing revolution in scientific fields like cosmology, quantum physics and biology: we are entering a new enlightenment, and Big Philosophy is where it is all coming together.

Client: Zembla
Design: Frost*
Technical overview:
Woodtype form with text
reversed out

BIG PHILOSOPHY by Alexander Bard

Philosopher, lecturer, author, music composer, producer, pop star and Scandinavia's most successful breeders of trotting horses, Bard is clearly a man of many talents. His first book, *Netocracy*, a meta-historical treatise which argues that historical shifts are determined by major revolutions in information technology, was an international bestseller. After studying the ancient Zoroastrian religion of Iran and India for seven years, Bard became only the second Westerner to convert to Zoroastrianism in 1993.

september_two thousand and three zembla magazine [103]

Silk-screen printing | Letterpress printing | Hot-metal printing

Zembla

This is a double-page spread from *Zembla* magazine, which was created by Frost*. The design was created using a letter character that was letterpress printed from a wood block, which was then digitized and reproduced in offset lithography. The text is reversed out of the black ink to appear white.

Aqua-coloured stock

K
Y
M
C

Hot-metal printing

Hot-metal printing, also know as hot-type composition or cast metal, refers to the process of casting type in lines of molten metal.

Text is typed into a machine to produce a punched paper tape, which controls the characters that are cast by the casting machine. Hot-metal type allows the production of large quantities of type in a relatively inexpensive fashion.

Movable type is a method that uses single type characters, which are set in a block and printed. As each character is a single unit, it is 'movable' and so can be used again and again.

A piece of movable type.

A tray of movable type characters in a printer's workshop. All the characters in the tray correspond to a particular typeface.

Movable type characters that have been locked into position in a chase or metal frame to produce a printed page.

Gavin Martin Associates (opposite)

This is a change-of-address card produced by design agency NB: Studio for Gavin Martin Associates. The company had relocated to the Tea Building in Shoreditch, London. Hot-metal printing was used to leave a heavy imprint in an uncoated stock, which provided a subtle, but direct, connection to the printing profession of the client. Each card was individually stained with a tea ring to link to the printer's new location and make every one unique. The cards carried the credit 'Printed in England using Darjeeling. Brewed by NB: Studio'.

Gavin Martin Associates have moved...
Unit 4.05 The Tea Building
56 Shoreditch High Street
London E1 6JJ
T:020 7729 0091 F:020 7729 9872
www.gavinmartin.co.uk

Printed in England using Darjeeling
Brewed by NB Studio

Gavin Martin Associates have moved...
Unit 4.05 The Tea Building
56 Shoreditch High Street
London E1 6JJ
T:020 7729 0091 F:020 7729 9872
www.gavinmartin.co.uk

Printed in England using Darjeeling
Brewed by NB Studio

Gavin Martin Associates have moved...
Unit 4.05 The Tea Building
56 Shoreditch High Street
London E1 6JJ
T:020 7729 0091 F:020 7729 9872
www.gavinmartin.co.uk

Printed in England using Darjeeling
Brewed by NB Studio

Gavin Martin Associates have moved...
Unit 4.05 The Tea Building
56 Shoreditch High Street
London E1 6JJ
T:020 7729 0091 F:020 7729 9872
www.gavinmartin.co.uk

Printed in England using Darjeeling
Brewed by NB Studio

Letterpress printing | **Hot-metal printing** | Thermography

C M Y K   Aqua-coloured stock

Thermography

Thermography is an in-line print finishing process that is used to produce raised lettering on paper substrates.

Thermographic powder is deposited on to a sheet of printed paper (from an offset press) while the ink is still wet. The powder sticks to the wet ink, and fuses to it when the substrate is passed through an oven, which leaves a raised surface with a mottled texture, as seen in the detail below. The process can also be used with letterpress printing.

Lisa Pritchard Agency (above and opposite)

This is a Christmas card created by SEA Design for the Lisa Pritchard Agency. The text has been thermographically printed to provide raised, 'bubbly' characters that are highly visible, very tactile and reflect light in a unique way.

SEASONS GREET
INGS FROM RICH
ARD BRADBURY/
NICK DALY/IGOR
EMMERICH/LAUR
ENCE HASKELL/N
ANCY HONEY/TO
NY MCGEE

LPA/

Client: Lisa Pritchard Agency
Design: SEA Design
Technical overview:
Thermographic printing to give
raised, mottled characters

Hot-metal printing | **Thermography** | Lino-cut printing

C M Y K Aqua-coloured stock

Lino-cut printing

Lino cut is a low-volume, relief-printing method in which an image is cut into a thin piece of linoleum that is inked and mounted on to a piece of wood. The wood is then pressed against a substrate, and must be re-inked for every impression. The method was used by artists Henri Matisse and Pablo Picasso.

The image cut out of the linoleum is the reverse, or mirror image of the desired final design. The lino cut is in essence the negative from which the positive is printed.

Paw Prints (opposite)

This is the cover of an illustrated, self-published book called Paw Prints, which was produced by design studio Webb & Webb. The red stripes on the cover and the book's illustrations were printed using the lino-cut method. The typography was reproduced by letterpress and the cover substrate is duplexed with a combination of paper board and endpapers. Lino-cut printing produces a unique impression each time due to the variations in ink-film thickness and application pressure.

Client: Self Published
Design: Webb & Webb
Technical overview:
Combination of lino-cut and
letterpress printing

P A W P R I N T S

A Story by Holly Skeet
Pictures by Chris Brown

Hand & Eye Editions

Thermography | **Lino-cut printing** | Industry view: Thomas Manss & Company

Aqua-coloured stock

C M Y K

Industry view: Thomas Manss & Company

Pictured are images of the beautifully produced collection of work by Korean artist Minjung Kim, best known for her layered paintings of rice paper.

Can you elaborate on the relationship between artist, designer and printer?
We believe that an artist's monograph is not simply a collection of text and images, where the designer is required to lay out content and make the composition look pretty.

There is an important story to be told and therefore a precision in the information contained. The designer must first understand in depth the artist's work. The story can be expressed in many ways, for example, through materials and finishings which is where the printer comes into play. Artists experiment and often combine techniques, pushing their ability to the limit. We ask the printers that we work with to follow and trust us, because we do the same with our design.

Can print and finish techniques add value and create a point of difference, difficult to create in any other way?
Of course they can, materials make a lot of difference. Almost the same difference there is between looking at a photograph of a painting and looking at the painting itself. They have the ability to inject life into a publication. We are bombarded everyday by images and sight is probably our weakest sense. We often forget that we don't simply read or look at books, we hold and touch them and this sense can be far more powerful and reliable than sight.

Thomas Manss & Company are a multidisciplinary design consultancy with offices in London, Berlin, Cesena and Rio de Janeiro. They have garnered a reputation for sensitive, well considered work in the corporate, arts and cultural sectors.
www.manss.com

The cover of the catalogue contains only the title, teasing viewers in.

Lino-cut printing | Industry view: Thomas Manss & Company

Aqua-coloured stock

C M Y K

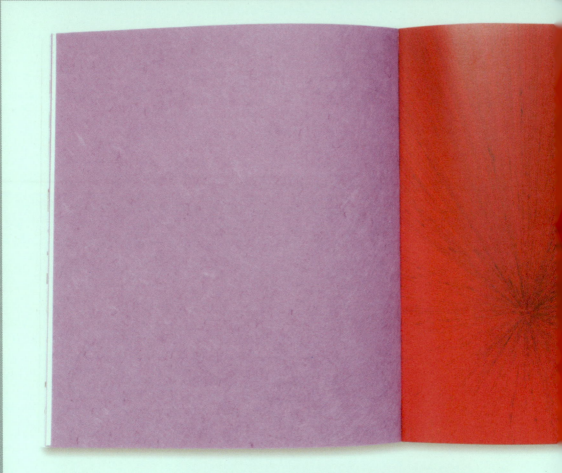

Handmade paper
was carefully ironed,
sheet by sheet,
before being wrapped
into sections!

Can paper selection, printing techniques and finishing methods be used to help tell the 'story' of a design?

If you are working with an artist, for instance, firstly you must learn and understand as much as you can about their work. Once the story to be told is clear, the tools that you have as your ally are: materials, printing, finishing techniques and binding.

Minjung Kim's work is incredibly original, it spans from watercolour to rice paper burning to sculpture. The catalogue that we have designed for her focusses mainly on the latter two. It was clear from the beginning that as designers we had to understand her work, the meaning, the feelings she wants to awaken and technically how she achieved all of this.

For instance, the title she had chosen for the book was '*Fire is Science and Sculpture*'. We decided to place it only on the title page, allowing the cover to tease the reader in. Hence the colour and texture of the material and the black foil. The cover is very tactile, the paper is handmade in France, emulating the look and feel of rice paper, and is the colour of fire. The endpaper and spine are orange, an unusual combination to reinforce the juxtaposition of tension and joy in her work. Once inside, each section introduces a different series and is wrapped in the same rice paper that she uses in her work. The paper arrived direct from Korea.

Lino-cut printing | **Industry view: Thomas Manss & Company**

Aqua-coloured stock

C M Y K

Client: Coast
Design: Frost*
Technical overview:
Blind deboss business cards

Chapter 3
Finishing

Print finishing encompasses a wide range of processes that can provide the final touches to a design once the substrate has been printed. These processes include die cutting, embossing, debossing, foil blocking, varnishing and screen printing to name but a few, and can transform an ordinary looking piece into something much more arresting.

Finishing processes can add decorative elements to a printed piece, such as the shimmer of a foil block, or textural qualities, such as those produced by an emboss or deboss. Finishing techniques can also provide added functionality to a design, and even be a constituent part of a publication's format. For example, a die cut alters the physical product, perhaps changing its shape or providing an aperture through which other parts of the publication can be viewed.

Although the application of print-finishing techniques signals the end of the production process, these techniques should not be considered as afterthoughts, but as an integral part of a design, and one that needs to be considered during the planning stage.

Coast (opposite)
These business cards by Frost*, for restaurant Coast, feature a blind deboss, strategically placed on the horizon of the image. The accompanying invitation can be seen on page 85.

Varnishes

A varnish is a colourless coating that is often applied to a printed piece to protect the substrate from scuffing, wear or smudging. Varnish can also be used to enhance the visual appearance of a design, or elements within it. Varnish can produce three finishes – gloss, dull and satin – and, while not strictly a varnish, UV coating can also be used to add decorative touches to designs.

Applying a varnish increases colour absorption and speeds up the drying process. By 'locking in' the printing ink under a protective coat, the varnish helps to prevent the ink rubbing off when the substrate is handled.

Varnish can be applied in-line or 'wet'; which essentially means it is treated as an additional colour during the printing process. A wet layer of varnish is applied on to a wet layer of ink, and both are absorbed into the stock as they dry, which reduces the visual impact of the varnish. An off-line varnish is applied once the printing inks have dried, and therefore less is absorbed by the stock. Varnish performs better on coated substrates, again because less is absorbed by the stock.

Varnishes can be used to produce different effects; as these details (above and opposite) taken from examples on the following pages, demonstrate.

Above, left to right: spot UV, clear and pearlescent varnishes.

Opposite, left to right: spot UV, lamination and black varnish.

Gloss

A gloss varnish reflects back light and is frequently used to enhance the appearance of photographs or other graphic elements in brochures, as it adds to the sharpness and saturation of images.

Matt (or dull)

A matt varnish is typically used with text-heavy pages to diffuse light, reduce glare and so increase readability. It gives a non-glossy, smooth finish to the printed page.

Satin (or silk)

A satin varnish is a middle option between the gloss and matt varnishes. It provides some highlight, but is not as flat as a matt finish.

Neutral

Machine sealing is the application of a basic, almost invisible, coating that seals the printing ink without affecting the appearance of the job. It is often used to accelerate the drying of fast turnaround print jobs (such as leaflets) on matt and satin papers, upon which inks dry more slowly.

UV varnish

UV varnish is a clear liquid that is applied like ink and cured instantly with ultraviolet light. It can provide either a gloss or matt coating. Increasingly, UV varnish is used as a spot covering to highlight a particular image because it provides more shine than varnish.

Full-bleed UV

The most common type of all-over UV coating, largely because it produces a very high gloss effect.

Spot UV

The varnish is applied to highlight discrete areas of a printed design, both visually and by imparting a different texture. The effect of spot UV can by maximized when it is applied over matt-laminated printing.

Textured spot UV

Textures can be created with spot UV varnish to provide an additional tactile quality to a print piece. Examples of textured spot UV varnish effects include sandpaper, leather, crocodile skin and raised.

Pearlescent

A varnish that subtly reflects myriad colours to give a luxurious effect.

Varnishes | Die cut

Woodfree uncoated

C M Y K

Client: Marsh Mercer
Design: Turnbull Grey
Technical overview:
Text reversed out of a
pearlescent varnish that retains
ease of legibility

AN INVITATION TO

FOURTH ANNUAL D

ON THE 23 FEBRUAR

AT THE HOLBEIN ST

FRANKELIDE

Client: E A Shaw
Design: Simplify
Technical overview:
UV spot varnish grid of initials

BE MOVED

Varnishes | Die cut

E A Shaw (above)
This brochure was designed by Simplify for London estate agent
E A Shaw. The cover of the brochure features a UV spot varnish of the lower
case 'i' and 'h' initials of the property development project name (Ingram House),
which were arranged in a grid pattern against a plain red background. The effect
is subtle yet eye-catching.

Marsh Mercer (opposite)
This invitation was created by Turnbull Grey design studio for risk specialist
Marsh Mercer. It features text which is printed in a pearlescent varnish and can
only be read clearly when it catches the light in a certain way. The main text
elements are printed in a slab-serif type and a large point size to facilitate reading.

Woodfree uncoated

K
Y
M
C

Client: RSA
Design: Untitled
Technical overview:
Clear varnish and emboss
to create tactile surface

Art for Architecture (right)

This is an invitation created by Untitled design studio for the Art for Architecture annual event, which is hosted by the Royal Society of Arts in the UK. The invitation features a black varnish that is applied in a halftone pattern on to a black substrate, which produces a very striking and arresting result.

Outside (left)

This is an invitation produced for the Royal Society of Arts by Untitled design studio. The design is screen printed on to greyboard stock, embossed and given a clear varnish coating. The varnish gives the screen print extra prominence and highlights the contrasting rough texture of the board, while giving a tactile difference in the surface.

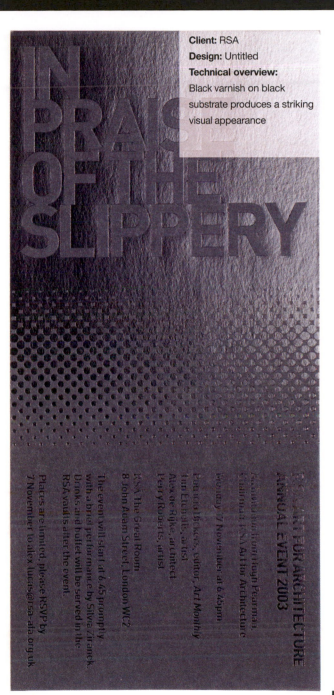

Client: RSA
Design: Untitled
Technical overview:
Black varnish on black substrate produces a striking visual appearance

Varnishes | Die cut

Woodfree uncoated

C M Y K

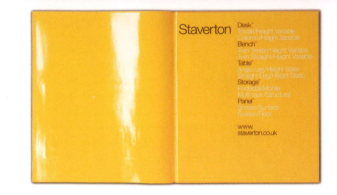

Staverton

Desk˝
Trestle/Height Variable
Columns/Height Variable
Bench˝
Twin Trestle/Height Variable
Twin Straight/Height Variable
Table˝
Spar Leg/Height Static
Straight Leg/Height Static
Storage˝
Pedestal/Mobile
Multi-task/Structural
Panel˝
Screen/Surface
Screen/Floor

www.
staverton.co.uk

Staverton

This brochure was created by SEA Design for office furniture company Staverton.
The brochure is laminated, which gives it a high-gloss effect. Shown below is an
impressive four-panel gatefold that the brochure contains.

Lamination

Laminate is a thin film that is applied to one or both sides of a printed stock. Lamination provides a range of
benefits, which include gloss or lustre, improved sheet stability or rigidity, and protection from moisture and
handling. Lamination can also make documents waterproof, tear-proof and tamper-proof.

Client: Staverton
Design: SEA Design
Technical overview:
Lamination provides high-gloss
effect and added protection

Varnishes | Die cut

Woodfree uncoated

C M Y K

Die cut

Die cutting is a process that uses a steel die to cut away a specified section of a design. It is mainly used for decorative purposes and to enhance the visual performance of a piece.

In addition to altering the shape of a design for visual enhancement, a die cut can serve a functional purpose such as creating an aperture that allows a user to see inside or through a publication.

The cards (left) are part of the Acorn project shown on the facing page, and share the same floral motif. The cards have die-cut rounded corners, which both softens their visual appearance and replicates the generous curves of the upper case 'A' in the main design.

Acorn (above and opposite)

These designs were created by Studio Output for conceptual textiles company Acorn. A die cut in the cover in the shape of an upper case 'A' (for Acorn) provides a view of the material inside, and this lends the piece depth and texture as the colours from the interior sheets are seen through the aperture. The die-cut cover reflects the floral theme of the content as the counter of the 'A' is designed as a sprig of leaves. The inner sheets are softened, in line with the floral themes they display, as they incorporate die-cut rounded corners.

Client: Acorn
Design: Studio Output
Technical overview:
Die-cut cover design and page
corners, flower theme
incorporated throughout

Acorn

Spring + Summer Collection '05
Conceptual Textiles

Varnishes | **Die cut** | Throw outs

Woodfree uncoated

C M Y K

Client: British Council
Design: Studio Myerscough
Technical overview:
Die cut gives shape of
cover element

nine positions
curated by peter cook
british pavilion
the 9th venice biennale
of architecture 2004

cj lim

Nine Positions (above)
This is a brochure that was created by Studio Myerscough for Nine Positions
an exhibition curated by Peter Cook for the ninth Venice Biennale of Architecture.
The publication is die cut so that it takes the shape of the stem of the yellow '9'
which is printed in a stencil font on the greyboard cover.

Museon (opposite)
This is a greetings card created by Faydherbe / De Vringer (Wout de Vringer)
design studio, which Dutch museum Museon gave to its staff. The circle die cut
provides an aperture through which one can view a coin mounted inside. The
coin commemorates the 750th anniversary of The Hague, and features an image
of the museum. Removal of the coin reveals the museum's logo.

Client: Museon
Design: Faydherbe / De Vringer (Wout de Vringer)
Technical overview: Die-cut aperture inspired by company identity

MUSEON

Varnishes | **Die cut** | Throw outs

Woodfree uncoated

C M Y K

Throw outs
A throw out is a folded sheet of paper that is bound into a publication to provide extra space to showcase a particular image or visual element.

To open a throw out, the extra panel is extended horizontally. The sheet will have a slightly smaller dimension than the overall publication so that it can nest comfortably when folded. A throw out is similar to a throw up (shown below right), which when opened is extended vertically.

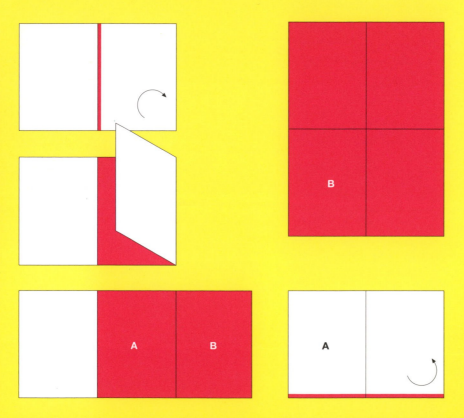

Left: A throw out; the recto page is a double panel page (A and B), which is folded into the spine of the publication. For panel B to nest comfortably in the publication it has to be slightly narrower than panel A. Panel A is narrower than the publication size so that the throw out will not be damaged during the binding and trimming processes. Right: A throw up sees the spread (A) open up vertically to reveal the concealed content (B).

Client: Blueprint Magazine
Design: George & Vera
Technical overview:
Two-page throw out

Will Alsop
Wilkinson Eyre
ZEDfactory
Future Systems
Eric Kuhne
Ben Kelly
Shin and Tomoko Azumi
Jane Atfield
Priestman Goode
Gerry McGovern
Seymour Powell
Jonathan Ive
Lisa-Dionne Morris
Craig Johnston
George Davies
Ross Lovegrove
Garrick Hamm
Mark Farrow
Martin Lambie-Nairn
Margaret Calvert
David Quay and Freda Sack

Die cut | **Throw outs** | Folding

Woodfree uncoated

C M Y K

Blueprint Magazine

This insert was created by George & Vera design studio for *Blueprint Magazine*. It features the work of creatives from a variety of design disciplines, including Margaret Calvert's UK motorway signage scheme, David Quay's and Freda Sack's Yellow Pages typeface design and Jonathan Ive's iPod design. The insert includes a two-page throw out.

Folding

Different folding methods will produce different creative effects and offer different functionality and means of organization.

Valley fold   **Mountain fold**

The valley and mountain folds (shown above) are both named after the geographical features they replicate. Both feature a single central fold. Combined, these two folds form the basis of a wide variety of fold combinations as shown on pages 80–89.

**Almeida Theatre
by NB: Studio**
This invitation for the Almeida Theatre features two die cuts that are perpendicular to the mountain fold. This folding method is called parallel folding, and in this instance the parallel fold helps create a seat for the die-cut figure

Client: Arnolfini
Design: Thirteen
Technical overview:
Irregular diagonal folds to
create three-dimensional
invitation

ARNOLFINI

Arnolfini

This is an invitation created by design studio Thirteen for the reopening of
Bristol's Arnolfini Gallery following an 18-month closure for architectural
redevelopment. The invitation is produced from a single leaf of Think4 stock that
is printed in four colours and has irregular diagonal valley and mountain folds,
which produces a three-dimensional object.

Throw outs | **Folding** | French fold

Woodfree uncoated

C M Y K

French fold

A French fold is a sheet of stock that is printed on one side and folded vertically and then horizontally to form a four-page uncut section.

A French fold can also be bound into a printed item (as shown in the illustration below) to give a more substantial feel to the publication's pages. The section is sewn through the (open) binding edge so that the fore- and top edges remain folded and untrimmed. The top edge (A) is trimmed off during the binding process to leave a sealed fore-edge that forms a cavity. The section inner may be printed on.

This standard French fold forms an eight-page section.

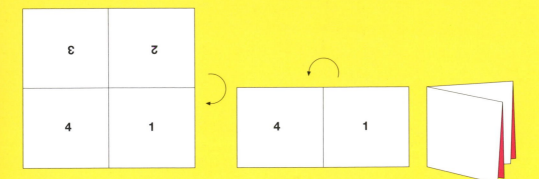

Heavily-filled or coated stocks are prone to cracking on the fore-edge and high-caliper stock may also crack when folded; this makes them unsuitable for French folding. This publication was created by North design studio. The content prints in the cavities of the French fold pages and the publication is printed on bible paper, a stock that will not crack when folded, and will lie flat.

Client: Sweeps
Design:
Studio Myerscough
Technical overview:
French fold doubles the
caliper of the page

Sweeps

This is a property brochure created by Studio Myerscough for the Sweeps
Building development in London's Clerkenwell area. The brochure features
French fold pages that add depth and substance to the publication.

This French fold will be perfect bound to create pages that have a cavity.

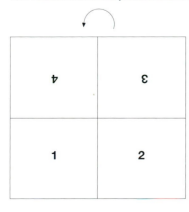

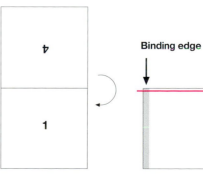

Binding edge

(A)

C M Y K   Matt art

Endorse folding

An endorse fold is a simple but effective way of finishing a publication. A printed and bound (usually saddle-stitched or loose-leaf) document is folded in half, reducing size and creating a more informal presentation.

An endorse fold is usually a non-mechanical fold. It is usually applied after the main binding and print run, and simulates the way one would fold an oversized newspaper. As it is a non-mechanical fold, the final endorse fold is usually not creased or pressed in any way, as the example opposite demonstrates.

Endorse folds are generally applied for aesthetic reasons, however there can also be economic reasons for doing this. By folding a publication in half, although the weight doesn't change, the dimensions halve. This can be useful where the size of a document has an impact on postage and or packaging costs.

Client: Central Saint Martins

Design: Studio Thomson

Technical overview:

Replacing binding with an endorse fold helps to keep costs down

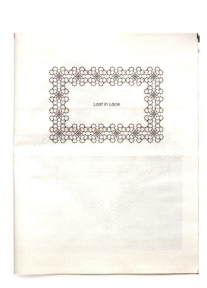

Lost in Lace

This newsprint publication for the Central Saint Martins foundation fashion and textiles course uses a traditional newspaper endorse fold. The project was financed by the students, and as such this offers a creative and cost effective option – the loose-leaf pages are collected and folded, with no need for additional binding or expense.

Matt art

K
Y
M
C

CMYK

Concertina fold

A concertina (or accordion) fold comprises two or more parallel folds that go in opposite directions and open out. This folding method enables many pages to be collapsed into a smaller size publication.

A concertina-folded document can be opened from either the left or right side. As a reader can open a concertina folded document at any point, the content needs to be coherent both when it is opened out and as a separate series of spreads.

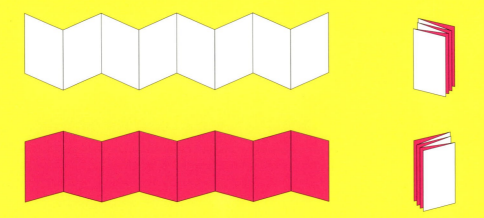

This illustration shows the alternating valley and mountain folds of a concertina fold, and how the size of the publication is reduced when folded.

Coast Restaurant (opposite)

This is an invitation which was created by Frost* design for restaurant, Coast. The 18-page publication features a concertina fold that turns the publication into a structure. It features delicate atmospheric photography, with the typography playfully interacting with the horizon of the image.

Client: Coast
Design: Frost*
Technical overview:
Concertina invitation with
delicate, coloured
photography

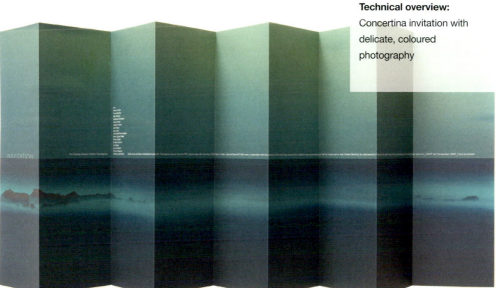

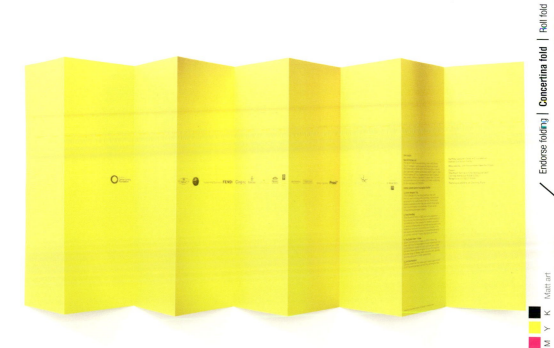

Endorse folding | **Concertina fold** | Roll fold

Matt art

C M Y K

Roll fold

A roll fold is composed of a series of parallel valley folds, which are further folded in to one another.

As the reader opens a roll-folded document, the content is gradually revealed panel by panel. In this way, the fold functions like a slow reveal. For a large document or rigid substrate, the panels may need to be of successively larger widths so that they can nest comfortably.

However, as with a concertina fold, the content contained within a roll-folded piece needs to read as a series of spreads in addition to a continuous strip. Roll folds can be used to good effect as a frieze graphic as the opened-out example below shows.

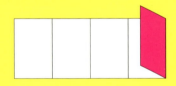

The document comprises a strip with several panels. Successive parallel valley folds are performed so that the document rolls up.

Christmas Card (above and opposite)
This card, 'stocking fillers', was created by Turnbull Ripley design studio.
It features seven black-and-white photographs of pairs of legs. The photographs are enclosed and hidden by a roll fold so that only the metallic gold outer is immediately visible. To view the photographs the reader unrolls the publication like a stocking is unrolled.

Client: Self published
Design: Turnbull Ripley
Technical overview:
Roll fold to conceal content

TURNBULL
RIPLEY
DESIGN
LEGENDS

Can you identify the Turnbull Ripley Legends?

For your chance to win an exclusive Turnbull Ripley
stocking packed full with festive goodies
simply match a number to a name and email your
line up to:

competition@turnbullripley.co.uk

The correct answer for the one who gets the most
right by 12.00pm on Friday 22nd December will be
emailed the winning line up.

Good luck and a very merry Christmas and a happy
new year from Mark, Tom, Greg, John, David, Vickie,
Dario, Nim, John-Paul, Paula, Daniel and Sean.

12 Stocking fillers from Turnbull Ripley

12 Stocking fillers from Turnbull Ripley

Concertina fold | **Roll fold** | Gatefold

C M Y K Matt art

Gatefold

A gatefold is a sheet with four panels that is placed in the publication so that the left and right panels fold inward with parallel folds and meet at the spine without overlapping.

In the illustration below, the inner panels (B) have the same dimensions of the publication, but the outer panels (A) are slightly narrower so that they can nest comfortably at the spine. Gatefolds are often used in magazines to provide extra space and are particularly useful for displaying panoramic vista images.

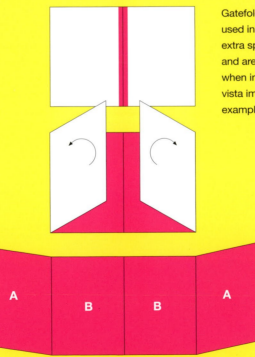

Gatefolds are commonly used in magazines to provide extra space to a key image, and are particularly useful when including panoramic vista images, as in the example opposite.

Gateway 241

Shown is a gatefold spread from a brochure for a building development in Sydney. One of the development's key features is its prominent position at Sydney's international gateway, which has 360° views of the city.

The simple, carefully considered exterior creates a contemporary identity for the development. Internally, the brochure features a double gatefold celebrating the panoramic views.

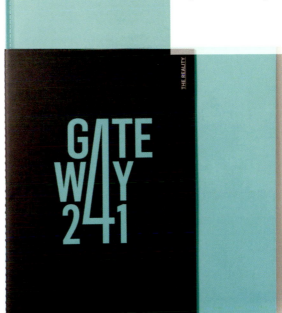

Client: Gateway 241
Design: Frost*
Technical overview:
Gatefold creating a sense of panoramic beauty

Roll fold | **Gatefold** | Embossing and debossing

C M Y K   Matt art

Embossing and debossing

An emboss or deboss is a design that is stamped into a substrate with ink or foil, which results in a three-dimensional, raised, decorative or textured surface to provide emphasis to certain elements of a design. Generally, a paper stock with a thicker caliper holds an emboss (or deboss) much better than thinner stocks.

Embossing
A raised impression made in conjunction with ink or foil on the embossed image.

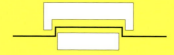

Blind embossing
A raised impression made without using ink or foil on the embossed image.

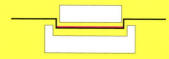

Debossing
A recessed impression made in conjunction with ink or foil on the debossed image.

Blind debossing
A recessed impression made without using ink or foil on the debossed image.

30/30 Vision (opposite)

This cover was created by Turnbull Grey design studio for 30/30 Vision: Creative Journeys in Contemporary Craft, an event held by the UK's Crafts Council. The cover features an abstract floral pattern made from small debossed circles.

Client: Crafts Council
Design: Turnbull Grey
Technical overview:
Abstract pattern with
debossed circles

Gatefold | **Embossing and debossing** | Foil blocking

Client: Vertigo Lounge

Design: Simplify

Technical overview:

Embossed logotype onto
coloured stock

Vertigo Lounge (above)

These menus feature an embossed, geometric, logotype that creates a strong
visual statement and forms an important part of the brand's overall identity.

Crafts Council (opposite)

This is the cover of a calendar that was created by Turnbull Grey design studio
for the UK's Crafts Council. The cover features a deep deboss into a flock
substrate, which is complemented by a silver foil block for the lettering.

Client: Crafts Council
Design: Turnbull Grey
Technical overview:
Deboss into flock with silver
foil block lettering

CRAFTS COUNCIL
THE NATIONAL CENTRE FOR CONTEMPORARY C

Gatefold | **Embossing and debossing** | Foil blocking

Client: Brookfield MG
Design: Simplify
Technical overview:
Graphic coloured emboss

rethink

redefine

enew

Client: Gumberg Global
Design: Poulin + Morris
Technical overview: Design
embossed into white board

GUMBERG GLOBAL

Gumberg Global (above)
Adding texture through embossing can enhance the overall brand and visual representation of a company. Here, a simple shape is used to convey a sense of global connectivity and dynamic activity. This exemplifies the understated beauty a blind emboss can convey.

Brookfield MG (opposite)
Brookfield MG are a company helping to transform buildings into greener, healthier workspaces. The company's green credentials are reflected with this bold, confident graphic statement.

Matt art

K Y M C

C M Y K

Foil blocking

Foil blocking is a process whereby coloured foil is pressed on to a substrate via a heated die, which causes the foil to separate from its backing.

The foil is a thin polyester film containing a dry pigment. Several terms are used to describe this process including foil stamp, heat stamp, hot stamp, block print and foil emboss.

Flat stamping
A basic flat stamp that gives a slight raise above the surface and usually no impression on the reverse side of the substrate.

Multi-level stamping
A die created with different levels and textures that can produce elegant designs. Also called sculptured foil embossing, it provides eye-catching results, but is more expensive.

There also exist, though they can be hard to source, a series of patterned and holographic foils, that are sometimes referred to as pastel foils.

These are details taken from the introductory page of a brochure that was created for Maddison Business Systems by Turnbull Grey design studio. This page of the brochure features foil-blocked type on a blue stock, which results in attractive detailing that imparts a quality feel to the publication.

Client: Erik Penser
Bankaktiebolag
Design: Bedow
Technical overview:
White foil to case bound book

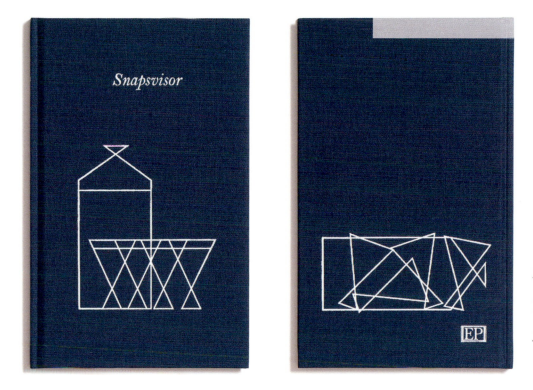

Snapsvisor

This gift book from a Swedish bank to their clients features a series of traditional drinking songs. Using a simple white foil, the design makes playful use of the front and the back of a book, to reflect the before and after of a drinks party.

Embossing and debossing | **Foil blocking** | Fore-edge printing

Gloss art

K
Y
M
C

Client: Wax Jambu
Design: Studio Output
Technical overview:
Bronze foil into uncoated,
recycled board

Wax Jambu (above)
Studio Output's strong visual identity for Wax Jambu creates a contrast of
textures and reflectivity

Hotel Skepsholmen (opposite)
Gabor Palotai's identity for Hotel Skepsholmen uses a deep, rich-coloured foil
to create a sense of modern luxury and style.

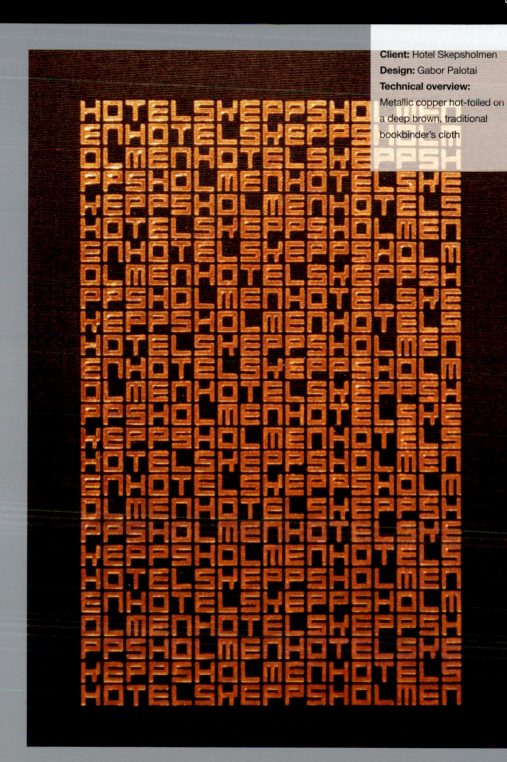

Client: Hotel Skepsholmen
Design: Gabor Palotai
Technical overview:
Metallic copper hot-foiled on a deep brown, traditional bookbinder's cloth

Embossing and debossing | **Foil blocking** | Fore-edge printing

Gloss art

C M Y K 877

Client: Andrew Hussey

Design: Andrew Hussey

Technical overview:
Copper orange foil onto
Colourplan stock

ndrewHussey

Multi-Disciplinary
Graphic Design

+44 (0)7764 7542

email@andrewhu

uk.linkedin.com

www.andrewh

Andrew Hussey (above)

This business card features a copper orange foil onto coloured board, creating tonal balance and intrigue. The use of a specific colour of foil can become as important a part of an identity as typeface or image selection.

Future Face (opposite)

This is the cover of Sandra Kemp's *Future Face*, which was designed by Studio Myerscough for Profile Books. The title of the book is emblazoned across a hyperreal image in an angular font that is silver-foil blocked, resulting in a very futuristic effect.

Client: Profile Books
Design: Studio Myerscough
Technical overview:
Silver-foil block title
provides futuristic effect

future
face

image
identity
innovation
sandra
kemp

Fore-edge printing | **Foil blocking** | Embossing and debossing | Gloss art

C M Y K

Fore-edge printing

Fore-edge printing uses a special process to print on the cut, outside edges of the book block of a publication. This process finds its origins in gilding, a process that applied gold or silver to the pages of a book to protect them but nowadays is used more commonly to add decorative effects.

This is a gold leaf fore-edge print taken from a publication created by dixonbaxi design studio. The project can be seen in full on page 171.

This black, fore-edge print was created by Studio Myerscough for Black Dog Publishing and homogenizes the pages with the cover, transforming the book into a seemingly solid object.

White Book (opposite)

This is the White Book, which was produced by SEA Design for paper merchant GF Smith, and contains details of the company's updated identity. A silver fore-edge print reflects light as the reader turns the pages, and complements the silver typography used. The book contains creative photographs of ink as can be seen on its cover.

Client: GF Smith
Design: SEA Design
Technical overview:
Silver fore-edge print
reflects light

Foil blocking | **Fore-edge printing** | Deckle edge

Gloss art

K 877

C M Y

Client: Parent
Design: Parent
Technical overview:
Copper foiled logo,
type and edging

urent.

Gloss art

K Y M C

Parent.
These business cards and letterheads are designed by and for design agency
Parent. They use a copper foil to create the logo, type and fore-edging to enhance
the identity and create a point of interest and tactile quality.

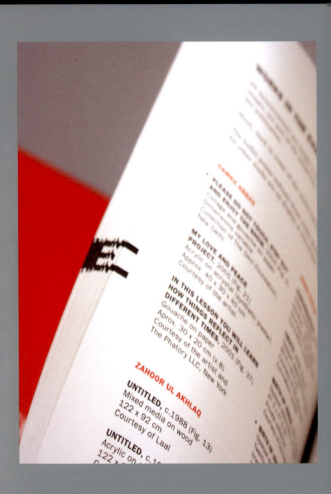

Beyond The Page

Reform Creative designed this brochure to accompany an exhibition which also included contributions from Roger Connah, Hammad Nasar, Anna Sloan and Virginia Whiles.

This document cleverly uses a form of psuedo-fore-edge printing. By incrementally moving a printed image on each page of the brochure, a fore-edge effect is created.

Client: Shisha
Design: Reform Creative
Technical overview:
Foil blocked cover with
fore-edge printing

Foil blocking | **Fore-edge printing** | Deckle edge

Gloss art

C M Y K 877

Deckle edge

A deckle (or feather) edge is the ragged edge of the paper as it leaves the papermaking machine. Machine-made paper has two deckle edges while handmade paper has four. When not cut away, the deckle edge can be used to great decorative effect. Equally, the effect can be imitated by tearing the edge of the paper by hand, as the example opposite shows.

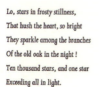

Lo, stars in frosty stillness,
That hush the heart, so bright
They sparkle among the branches
Of the old oak in the night!
Ten thousand stars, and one star
Exceeding all in light.

This spread is taken from The Wonder Night, a book of Christmas stamps designed by Irene von Treskow.

The Wonder Night (above and opposite)

This is a hand-produced, limited-edition book of Christmas stamps that was created by Webb & Webb design studio for Royal Mail. The stamps were designed by Irene von Treskow and depict scenes from 'The Wonder Night'; a poem by Laurence Binyon.

The pages feature a horizontal imitation deckle edge. This was produced by tearing off the edge of the paper and lends a handmade quality to the publication.

Client: Royal Mail
Design: Webb & Webb
Technical overview:
Handmade imitation
deckle edge

The Wonder Night

Fore-edge printing | **Deckle Edge** | Perforation

Gloss art

C M Y K

Perforation

Perforation (or perf cutting) is a process that creates a cut-out area in a substrate, which weakens it for detaching.

Perforations are made using perforating blades that can be shaped into a given pattern, so that the cut area of the blade slices through the stock, while the uncut segment (or tie) of the blade does not.

Mailer (above and opposite)

Pictured right is a mailer outer for a self-promotional piece for design studio George & Vera. As the brochure is perforated it can be mailed without the need to enclose it in a separate envelope. Simple printed instructions tell the user how to access the showcase of George & Vera's work, which is shown inside.

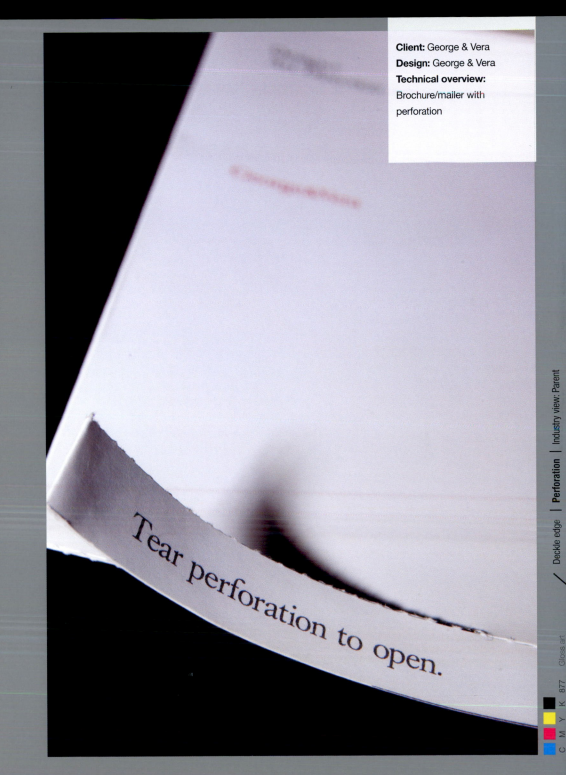

Client: George & Vera
Design: George & Vera
Technical overview:
Brochure/mailer with
perforation

Tear perforation to open.

Deckle edge | **Perforation** | Industry view: Parent

Gloss art

C M Y K 877

Industry view: Parent

Pictured over the following pages are examples of print finishing techniques adopted by Parent for property developer Silver Arrow.

Do you feel that print finishing techniques give the outcome added value?
Absolutely, I always use luxury cars as an analogy; in a well-built car, it's the fine details that add up to create a luxury product – the satisfyingly smooth draw that slides out, the solid thud of a well-built door closing or the happy click of a button. All those details work together to provide the feeling of quality and that's the difference between a luxury car people enjoying driving and talking about and a standard car nobody cares too much about. We see the printed details and finishes in the same way, it's those details that are the difference between a customer cherishing your business card or binning it. It increases the time people spend with the item and therefore increases the impact of the item and the brand it's come from.

How do you come to a decision on when it is appropriate to use print and finishing techniques?
Every job needs the same level of attention to the finishing details, it's just a case of using the most appropriate for the project, the brand and its market.

Parent are a design agency based on the south coast of the UK working with clients internationally. They specialize in branding design, strategy and communication. Working across a diverse range of sectors for a broad range of clients, Parent's work covers brand identity design and development, web and application design and development, design for print and advertising.
www.madebyparent.com

Pages die-cut at
converging angles create
a dynamic and tactile
brochure. This also creates
a sense of juxtaposition
between images.

Matt art

C M Y K

BESPOKE BUILD

Silver Arrow has witnessed an increase in demand for high quality residential bespoke build. Our experienced dedicated team offer a unique in house service that makes designing and building your own home to suit your requirements a very simple process - Without compromise!

[...] election of plots to choose from or our land buyer [...] our perfect plot. If you would like to find out [...] service we offer please call to make an [...] or to pop in for a friendly chat.

...desire can be achieved.

[...]d [...] bu[...] very [...] in a h[...] greater [...] property [...] the local r[...]

We have ma[...] relationship ar[...] now manage al[...] maintenance of t[...] gardening, even [...] housekeeping, even[...] a watchful eye over t[...] when we are away.

We truly have our dream[...] and without a doubt this is [...] to the efforts of the Silver A[...] team. A big thankyou.

Owen & Jennie
Owners of Destiny

Subtle details, including blue
stitching instill a sense of
care and craft in the designs.

Can you elaborate on the collaborative relationship between designer and printer?

For us, it's really important to involve our print partners early on in the process, their input can prove really valuable by being part of the process rather than just the end of it. It helps us to discover new ideas, processes and finishes we may not have thought of and helps us get the best out of a client's budget by working with the print team to find the right overall solution. We worked really closely with the guys at Opal when working on the Silver Arrow brochure to make sure we could achieve the cut pages at the right angles within a tight budget. Their help at the early stage meant we could add the singer sewn binding, which was really important to add the bespoke feel we were after.

Fore-edge printing to the sides of the business cards creates a strong architectural stance for the brand.

Client: Oskar de Kiefte
Design:
Faydherbe / De Vringer
(Wout de Vringer)
Technical overview:
Special varnish applied after
printing as final pass

Chapter 4
Production

The production processes used in graphic design and the printing industry, to physically put ink on paper, can be harnessed in many ways to produce creative results. These may include manipulating the colour channels and printing plates, overprinting or reversing out and changing the order in which the process colours print. The impact and creative potential of a design can be enhanced when you control the creative process, rather than letting it control you, as the following pages will show.

This book has sections that print with special colours adding graphic interest and a change in pace. Pages 17, 20, 21, 24, 25, 28, 29, 32 98, 99, 102, 103, 106, 107, 110, 111 for instance print with various metallic colours. Pages, 114, 115, 118, 119, 122, 123, 122 and 127 print with a fluorescent pantone colour, again adding a point of interest. There are also a variety of different stocks, both in terms of finish and colour that have been used throughout this book. The location of these can be seen on the imposition plan on page 27.

40% Auto

40% Auto is a book/catalogue created by artist Oskar de Kiefte, and designed by Faydherbe / De Vringer (Wout de Vringer). The design concept is based on that of a mail-order catalogue, and the artist's work is presented as products that can be purchased. The title reflects the fact that 40% of de Kiefte's projects involve cars. The book's cover is printed in black and red, with a special shiny varnish that overprints the red text to create a subtle two-tone effect. The red ink contains metallic silver to imitate the highly reflective nature of traffic signs, which glow when car headlights hit them.

Special colours

When we think of traditional lithographic printing (see pages 42–43) we tend to think of Cyan, Magenta, Yellow and Black, or CMYK. But the possibilities of colour reproduction are much greater than this.

Most lithographic printing presses are capable of running more than the four colours of the CMYK printing method. Special, or spot, colours include a range of tonal values that are impossible to replicate out of the four colours of lithographic printing. Shown below are two swatches. On the left, a spot colour, in this instance a fluorescent pink, and on the right, an assimilation of this out of the CMYK printing method. In converting to CMYK, the brightness and intensity of the colour is lost, as the colour is converted to a tint of magenta.

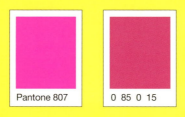

Pantone 807   0 85 0 15

Metallics
There are a series of metallics, as printed in this book on pages 17, 20, 21, 24, 25, 28, 29, 32, 98, 99, 102, 103, 106, 107, 110 and 111, that faithfully replicate the hues, tones and reflectivity of metals. Metallics use as their base, a silver and a bronze. By mixing these two colours, with for example orange, red, blue or green, you can create a wide range of alternative metallic colours.

Pastels
Special pastel colours are used to create very delicate flat colours, for example baby pinks and blues. If these colours are produced out of CMYK they are created using tints of colours (either cyan, magenta, yellow or black) and therefore appear with a visible dot, as opposed to the absolute flatness of the special or spot colour.

Client: Brandston
Partnership Inc
Design: Poulin + Morris
Technical overview:
Brochure/mailer with
perforation

Special **colours** | Rasters and **vectors**

Brandston Partnership Inc

A strong sense of identity can be created using a variety of graphic techniques;
a bold approach to typography, for example, or even just the confident use of a
fluorescent colour, in this case Pantone 810.

C M Y K 807

Rasters and vectors

Rasters (photographs) and vectors (illustrations) are the mainstay image formats of printed material today.

This image of a swimmer (shown above) is a raster file that, at this size, looks clear and of photographic quality. However, a limitation of the raster format is that it does not contain sufficient information to produce a clear image when enlarged, as pixelation begins to occur (A). In this context, pixels are also referred to as artefacts.

A raster file can be turned into a vector file for graphic effect. The picture on the opposite page has been enlarged, but as it is a vector file, even a large degree of upsizing produces recognisably sharp lines (B). However, remember that a poor quality raster image is still an image that does not contain enough information to be reproduced clearly. Rasters are turned into vectors for creative effect, not to solve resolution issues.

A

B

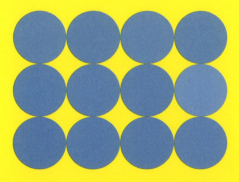

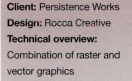

Client: Persistence Works
Design: Rocca Creative
Technical overview:
Combination of raster and
vector graphics

Open Studios

Friday 25 November 11am-4pm and special evening event with live music and
refreshments from 6pm-9pm.
Saturday 26 November 11am-5pm with copper beating workshops.

More information:
Yorkshire ArtSpace Society
Persistence Works
21 Brown Street
Sheffield
S1 2BS

t/t: 0114 276 1769
e: info@artspace.co.uk
w: www.artspace.org.uk

Special colours | **Rasters and vectors** | **Overprinting techniques**

Matt art

C M Y K

Overprinting techniques
Overprinting, surprinting and reversing out can all be used to great creative effect.

An overprint describes the printing of one colour on top of another. A surprint is where a percentage or tone of a colour is used; and a reverse out is where the white (or colour) of the page or substrate is used and the printed colour forms the background or base colour.

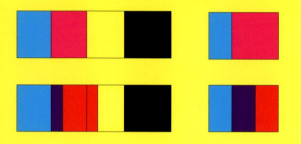

Knockout
The default setting on most software is for colours to knockout so that pure colours are preserved.

Overprint
Colour application can be set to overprint, which allows the colours to interfere with one another.

Knockout
A knockout is a gap that is left in the bottom ink layer so that an image printed over it (that overlaps it), appears without colour modification from the ink underneath it. The bottom colour is literally 'knocked-out' of the area where the other colour overlaps. To print a magenta circle on a cyan square, the cyan square must first be printed with a white circle (A). The hole in which the circle will print is slightly smaller than the magenta circle to be printed to avoid ink trapping issues (B). The magenta circle slightly overprints the blue square to avoid any white lines appearing due to misalignment of the two plates (C).

Ink trapping
Ink trapping is the overlapping of areas of coloured text or shapes to compensate for misregistration on the printing press. Ink trapping is required because the halftone dots that make up printed images overlap (because they are of different sizes and at different screen angles); therefore, the colours must also be overlapped to prevent the appearance of white gaps where they are supposed to meet.

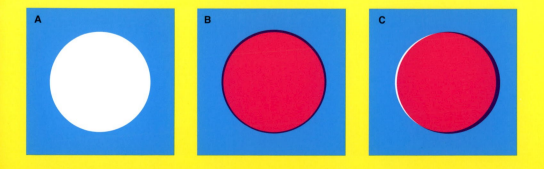

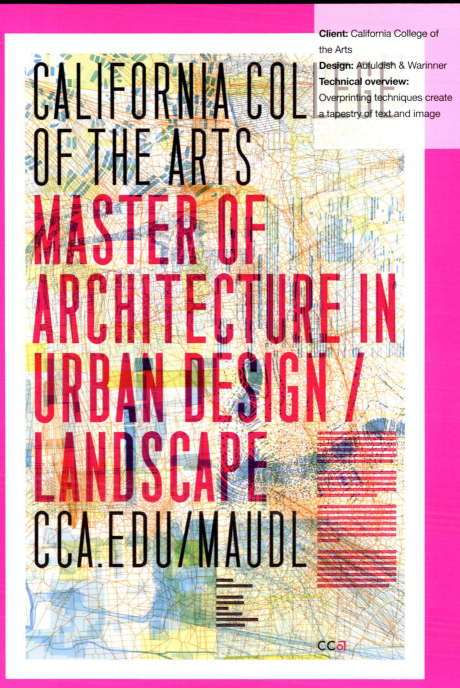

CALIFORNIA COLLEGE
OF THE ARTS
MASTER OF
ARCHITECTURE IN
URBAN DESIGN /
LANDSCAPE
CCA.EDU/MAUDL

Client: California College of the Arts
Design: Aufuldish & Warinner
Technical overview:
Overprinting techniques create a tapestry of text and image

Rasters and vectors | **Overprinting techniques** | Channels and plates

C M Y K 807 Match

California College of the Arts
Aufuldish & Warinner's design for the California College of the Arts uses layering and overprinting to create a tapestry of words and images.

Channels and plates

Most printed images are produced using a combination of the C, M, Y and K plates of the four-colour printing process.

Understanding the principles of how the four-colour process builds an image allows a designer to treat each colour pass separately, and in doing so obtain better colour adjustment and/or graphic interventions.

The four process inks are applied via separate printing plates in the cyan, magenta, yellow and black sequence in order to build up an image. Notice the difference that the addition of the black plate (K), makes to the image (left) compared to the C+M+Y version below.

C

C+M

C+M+Y

C+M+Y+K

This is the four-colour image, but with a lower amount of black.

This is the four-colour image with channels adjusted to create a warmer effect.

More and more extreme variants of colour can be introduced.

Rotating channels independently creates graphic interventions of colour and form.

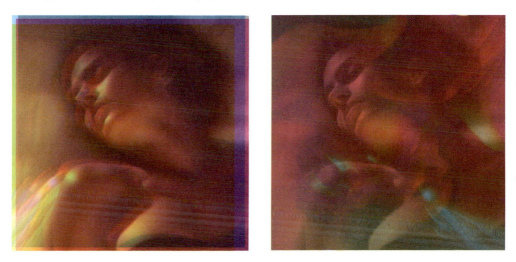

The colour channels in these images have been misregistered and rotated to produce different effects.

The levels and intensity of certain channels can be altered to create graphic interventions.

Overprinting techniques | **Channels and plates** | Halftones

Matt art

C M Y K

Client: This is a Magazine
Design: Andy Simionato
& Karen Ann Donnachie
(Donnachie, Siminonato
& Sons)
Technical overview:
Radical overprinting

This is a Magazine (above and opposite)
These are spreads taken from *This is a Magazine* use vector and raster image elements. The different components of the design overprint; creating a textured graphic tapestry of colour and form.

Channels and plates | **Overprinting techniques** | Halftones

Halftones

A halftone is an image composed of different-sized dots, which reproduce the continuous tones of a photograph.

The dots, which can be formed from various shapes, can be manipulated in terms of their size, spacing and screen angle, as the examples below illustrate.

This is the base image.

This image uses enlarged halftone dots.

The use of halftone lines produces a graphic effect.

The halftone lines in this image are at an angle, which provides a hatching effect.

Rather than dots, this halftone image is produced from ellipses.

This images uses halftone squares.

Zembla (opposite)

These spreads were created by Frost* for literary magazine *Zembla*. The image elements of the spreads have been rendered with a dot-shaped halftone effect.

Client: Zembla Magazine

Design: Frost*

Technical overview:

Dot-halftone rendered images

Tonal images

A tonal image is akin to a black-and-white photograph in which the white tones have been replaced by one of, or a combination of, the other CMY process colours.

Basic duotone produced using cyan and black.

Cyan flooding has been introduced to produce a darker effect.

Tritones generally produces a warming effect.

Flooded Pantone 807 duotone.

The colour curves on these duotones have been adjusted to give different intensity to the tonal colour.

Experimentation with the colour curves can produce very graphic results.

Client: Levi Strauss & Co.
Design: Morla Design
Technical overview:
Manipulated historical images, silk-screened chipboard cover, special colours and a dull varnish

Half tones | **Tonal images** | Industry view: Wout de Vringer

Gloss art

This is a pair of Levi's Jeans...

Part of the permanent collection of the San Francisco Museum of Modern Art, this brochure for Levi's celebrates the brand's 140-year history. Art director Jennifer Morla elaborates: 'the book lavishly illustrates the past 140 years of Levi's 501 jeans with over 300 pages of the people, places, movements and marketing that turned one brand into an American icon'. The book also features further printing enhancements through the use of a silkscreened chipboard cover, and the use of a dull varnish on the inner pages. The image treatments combine historical imagery with contemporary colourways and graphic treatments, simultaneously reflecting the brands heritage and modernity.

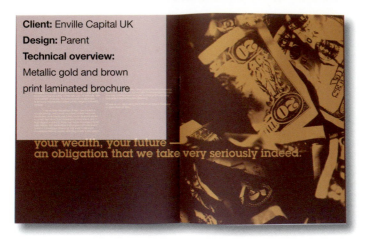

Client: Enville Capital UK

Design: Parent

Technical overview:

Metallic gold and brown
print laminated brochure

your wealth, your future —
an obligation that we take very seriously indeed.

a passionate desire to secure the future wellbeing
of yourself, your family and your interests.

Enville Capital UK

This brochure showcases the services of wealth management company Enville
Capital UK. It prints metallic gold and brown, colours that give a warm, refined and
opulent feel. This is enhanced by the spacious layout and spartan use of text
juxtaposed against full-bleed photography. The brochure is laminated to give the
stock additional substance and a more luxurious feel.

Client: Land Securities

Design: NB: Studio

Technical overview:

Highly-saturated, four-colour photographic and duotone images with gradient fade

Land Securities

This is a brochure created by NB: Studio for Land Securities for a series of property developments. Highly-saturated, four-colour photographic images are used to convey the 'love shopping' theme (pictured bottom) and these contrast sharply with the duotone images of the property developments. The duotones also feature a gradient fade from top to bottom.

Halftones | **Tonal images** | Industry view: Wout de Vringer

Gloss art

K

Y

M

C

Industry view: Wout de Vringer

Pictured is a catalogue for an exhibition 'Mapping the Landscape', held in the public domain in and around the city of Venlo.

Do you feel that print finishing techniques can give a sense of narrative and structure to a publication?
Absolutely! I believe if you make the right choice in print finishing techniques you can give an extra layer of meaning to your design. And in the case of this book, Mapping the Landscape, I used the precision of laser die-cut. When this technique was just around it was so expensive that I never had the chance to use it but now, some ten years later, it is much more affordable… And it fitted perfectly with what I had in mind for the design of the cover of the book.

Mapping the Landscape is a catalogue for an exhibition that was held in the public domain in and around the city of Venlo. Venlo is a town on the south-east border of The Netherlands with Germany. Dutch and German artists were invited to do projects that reflected the specific atmosphere that this border-town has. What you see in the picture of the cover is a kind of logo that shows, in a very schematic way, the city of Venlo and it's surroundings. The weight of the crosses depicts the amount of inhabitants in a certain area, and also stand for the way in which borders are depicted in maps.

This image played a very important role throughout the whole project. It was used on all the invitations, on the website, the lettering in the exhibition itself and it was used in all the maps pointing out where the artists have done their site-specific projects. It was more or less used as a corporate logo to make the people of Venlo familiar with this project called Mapping the Landscape.

Wout de Vringer (formerly of Faydherbe / De Vringer) is a graphic designer based in the Netherlands. Wout's extensive body of work has included cultural, academic, arts and theatre design.
www.woutdevringer.nl

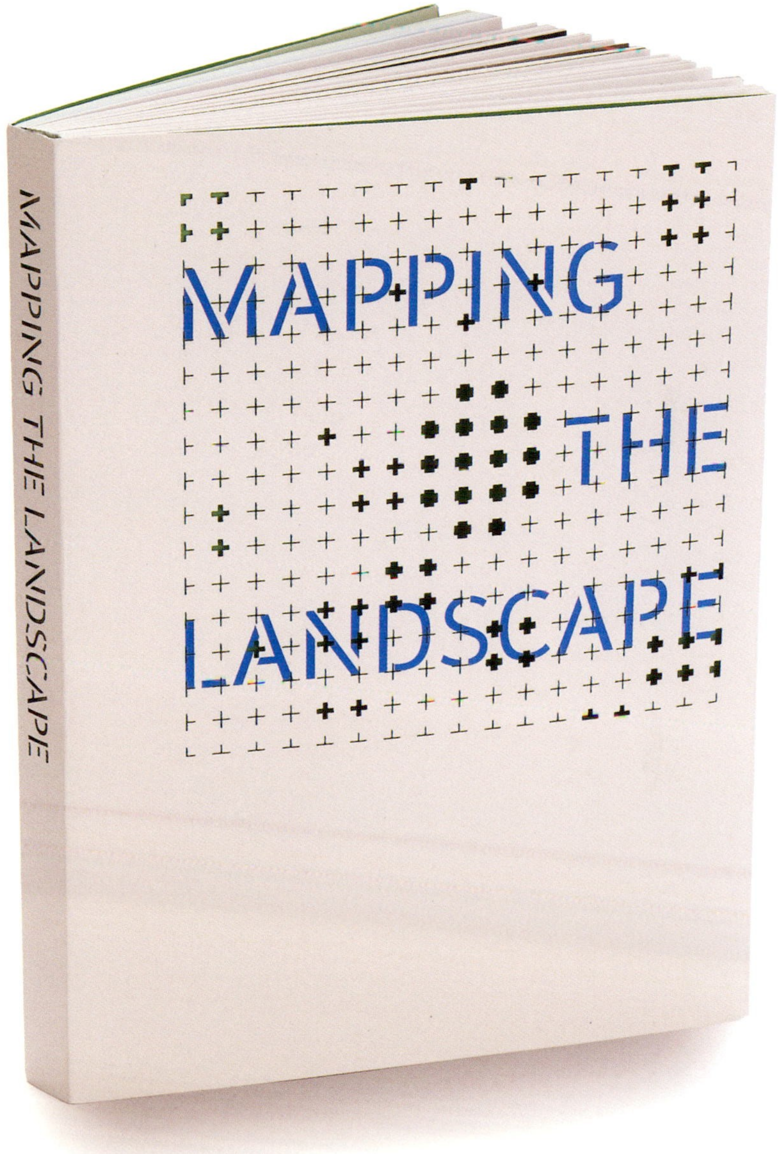

The laser-cut cover and spine
conceal a flood-colour, as shown
on the following spread.

Tonal images | **Industry view: Wout de Vringer**

Gloss art

C M Y K

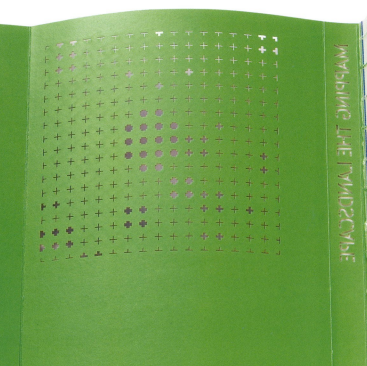

Pantone 3005 and Pantone
361 are used along with a
laser die cut to create a
strong visual identity for the
whole exhibition

MAPPING THE LANDSCAPE

Antoine Berghs
Paul Devens
Sebastian Freytag
Philippine Hoegen
Frank Koolen
Heidi Linck
Paulien Oltheten
Kai Rheineck

Museum van Bommel van Dam

Venlo 2012

Can you elaborate on the collaborative relationship between designer, artist and printer?
For over twenty years I have been working with the same guy who works as a print-consultant at a printer. Some years ago he changed jobs and started to work for another company. And so did I…

I really believe that one should cherish such a good and useful working relationship. He is very knowledgeable about print finishing techniques and all kinds of different paper stocks and effects. So when I select paper and decide on what print and finishing techniques I would like to use for a certain project, he gives me feedback and advice.

Lately, I have been working almost exclusively for cultural institutions, artists and publishers. Especially artists are very interested in all the different options you have in the actual printing process. Most of them like to join me when I go on a press-check… And I think it is a good idea to involve them in the whole process: from the first sketches until the final, printed piece…For them it is not just a catalogue or a brochure but it's a piece of their own life…

Tonal images | **Industry view: Wout de Vringer**

Gloss art

K
Y
M
C

Client: National Grid
Design: Simplify
Technical overview:
Elasticated diary band to
attach pencil and booklet

Chapter 5
Binding

Binding is the collective term for the range of processes that are used to hold together the pages or sections of a publication to form a book, magazine, brochure or other format. The different binding methods available allow a designer to make choices about the functionality of a publication in addition to its visual qualities, permanence and cost. Used creatively, binding can provide a simple means of differentiating a publication and adding a special touch.

Binding choices have a direct influence on the durability of a publication; sewn or burst binding are more durable methods than perfect binding, for example. Consumer magazines have a short shelf life and so saddle stitching or perfect binding is typically used as these methods are cheaper and their durability for the format is of less importance. If a publication needs to lie flat, which is often the case for manuals, wiro or Canadian binding is more appropriate.

Binding

Gloss art

National Grid Chairman's Awards (opposite)
This brochure for the National Grid Chairman's Award featured a series of puzzles and interactive games – thus necessitating a pencil. Simplify made use of a striking yellow coloured diary band to succinctly bring the elements together.

C M Y K

Open binds

Open binds offer an informal, industrial looking approach. Essentially, these bings are an un-covered, unfinished book, that create a strong graphic statement.

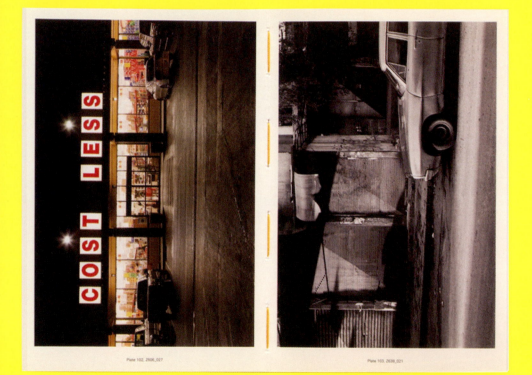

Millennium (above and opposite)

The book celebrating images from the Millennium picture library uses an exposed, or open bind to make a strong graphic statement. This contemporary publication prints on a series of white and off-white stocks, reflecting the cutting-edge photography within.

Client: Millennium
Design: Studio Thimson
Technical overview:
Sculptural book created using
an exposed, or open bind

The open bind allows the
book to be fanned out, creating
a sculptural statement.

Open binds | Wiro, spiral and comb binding

Gloss art

Wiro, spiral and comb binding

Wiro binding is characterized by a metal spine that passes through specially cut holes in the binding edge of a publication.

The main benefit of this binding method is that it allows the pages of the publication to lie flat, as can be seen in the example opposite. It also leaves the spine uncovered, as can be seen in the illustration below. Care needs to be taken with any images that cross the gutter of the document, where the punch-holes can interfere with the aesthetic.

Wiro binding
Opposed metal teeth 'bite' through holes that are cut in the pages, and meet to bind the pages.

Spiral binding
A metal spiral is fed, from the top to the bottom (or vice versa), through holes that are cut in the pages, to bind the publication. This process is more time consuming, but holds the pages more securely.

Comb binding
This follows the same principle as wiro binding, but uses a plastic comb rather than metal teeth.

Eurostar (opposite)
This is a brochure created by HGV Felton for rail company Eurostar. It has five wiro-bound leaves and 12 short, varnished tip-ins, which are used to represent the Solari analogue information display system that is used in airports and rail stations to convey information about flight or train times. The rich, atmospheric black-and-white imagery draws attention to the spine of the publication where the wire binding is used as the hinge in the message system, which invites the reader to interact with it.

Client: Eurostar

Design: HGV Felton

Technical overview:

Wiro binding with tip-ins
to represent information
display system

esprit europe is the leading supplier of courier services between central London and central Paris, and now Brussels. Esprit Europe has introduced a new dimension to the city courier business. Up to 20 Eurostar trains each day offer our Euro same-day delivery service, the innovative next day Euro by 9 service — a unique package of services. Our customers include some of the largest alongside some of the smallest companies in London — they all value the specialist service from Esprit Europe.

BRUSSELS

Canadian binding
Canadian binding takes two forms: Canadian and half-Canadian, although both methods are essentially the same.

Both Canadian and half-Canadian binding utilize a wiro, which is set within a wrap around cover to hold the pages of a publication together. Both methods allow the document to lie flat, and to have a spine to carry titling and volume information.

Full-Canadian bind
A Canadian or full-Canadian bind has a covered spine, as in the illustration shown below left.

Half-Canadian bind
A half-Canadian bind has notches in the cover that expose the spine, as in the illustration shown below right.

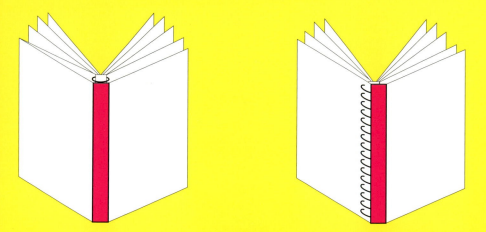

In this example, the text block (A) is Canadian bound to a base of the same size (B). This valley folds into two panels (C), which are large enough to hold it, and a cover spine (D), which allows the publication to be closed. All the folds are indicated in magenta.

C   D   C   B   A

Client: Arts Council England
Design: Untitled
Technical overview:
Canadian binding and die-cut corners

Necessary Journeys

This publication, which is a record of the physical and metaphorical journeys of a group of artists,was created by Untitled design studio for the Arts Council England. The publication uses full-Canadian binding, which consists of a wiro (spiral wire) set within a wraparound cover that encloses the spine so that the wire is not visible. The publication has die-cut corners that become progressively shorter to form a tabbing reference system for the pages.

Wiro, spiral and comb binding | Canadian bindig | Self binds

Green-coloured stock

K   C   M   Y

Self binds

Certain publications can appear to be bound, when in fact the only finishing process that has been used is folding.

Such publications are described as self binds because the reader manually rebinds the publication after using it by folding it again. Maps and brochures are typical examples of self binds.

This illustration is an example of a publication featuring an accordion fold in which the first two panels (highlighted in magenta) form a cover that the other panels fold into. The first two panels are larger than the others to allow for creep.

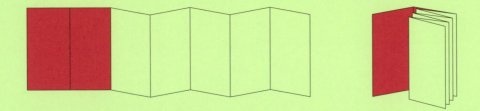

Situations Annual Report (below and opposite)

This annual report was created by Thirteen design studio on behalf of Situations. Launched in 2003, Situations set out to commission new art within a context of critical debate and discussion. This report summarizes the programme's diverse and cumulative impact to date. Instead of a formal binding for this 30-page publication, Thirteen chose to use an accordion fold. One side of the report provides factual information about audience figures, finances and funding while the other side presents the organization's vision, mission and information about its projects and publications. Printed in two parts and finished by hand, the pages incorporate subtle colour graduations to represent Situation's ability to change fluidly.

Client: Situations
Design: Thirteen
Technical overview:
Accordion fold that
contains all pages

Case binding

Case or edition binding is a durable method often used in the production of hardback books.

Vellum
Vellum is a translucent paper that is sometimes used to protect colour plates in a book. It is available in different patterns or textured effects such as linen.

Buckram
Buckram is a coarse linen or cotton fabric, sized with glue or gum, which is used for covering a hardcover binding.

Headbands and tailbands
Headbands and tailbands are pieces of cloth tape that cover the top and bottom of the spine for both decorative and protective purposes.

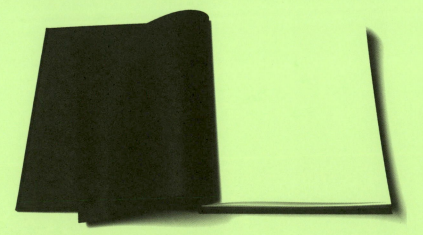

Endpapers
Endpapers are the sheets of heavy, cartridge-paper stock that are found at the front and back of a case-bound book, and which join the book block to the binding.

Client: Sergison Bates
Design: Cartlidge Levene
Technical overview:
Case-bound, buckram-
covered publication

Sergison Bates architects
Brick-work: gewicht und präsenz

Perfect binding

Case binding

Self binds

Green-coloured stock

C M Y K

Brick-work
This is Brick-work, a publication created by Cartlidge Levene design studio for
Sergison Bates architects. This case-bound book's title is screen-printed into
the buckram cloth covering.

Perfect binding

Perfect, or unsewn, binding is a method that is commonly used for magazines and paperback books.

To perfect bind a publication, the sections are formed into a block and the binding edge is glued with a flexible adhesive, which holds them together without the use of stitches and also attaches the cover.

The binding edge may sometimes be cut to allow the adhesive to have greater purchase, which is why the method is sometimes called cut-back binding. The fore-edge is then trimmed to give a clean, straight finish. The quality of the adhesive will determine how durable this binding is.

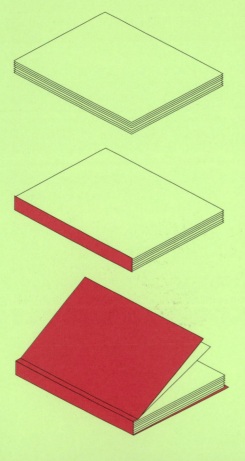

Perfect-binding process
The signatures are collated and formed into a book block. The spines are cut away or notched and adhesive is applied. A cover is then attached and folded around the book block. Finally, the fore-edge is trimmed. Notice that the spine edge is pinched.
In essence, the pinch acts as the fulcrum for page turning that gives the gutter space and prevents weakening the spine.

Section sewing
The sections of the book block can be thread sewn prior to being bound to give added strength, but this process takes longer and is consequently more expensive.

Thread sealing
This process combines perfect binding and section sewing but there is no thread running between the sections.

Side sewing
This method uses a thread that goes from the front to the back of the text block. It produces an extremely strong binding and therefore, unsurprisingly, it is often used in children's books.

Client: RSA
Design: Untitled
Technical overview:
Perfect-bound brochure with
emboss, deboss and die cut to
enhance black-on-black effect

RSA ART FOR ARCHITECTURE

RSA

This is the Art For Architecture brochure, which was produced for the Royal
Society of Architecture by Untitled design studio. The front cover features a black
stock that combines an embossed circle design with a die cut, which creates a
black-on-black effect that also adds texture to the piece. The back cover
features the artists whose work is contained in the brochure as a deboss.

Alternative bindings | **Perfect binding** | Case binding

Green-coloured stock

K
C M Y

Alternative bindings
Unusual techniques or materials can supply a range of creative binding effects.

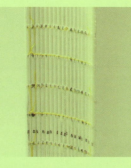

Open bind
An open bind has visible stitching; this example is by Tank design studio for Mind magazine.

Bellyband
This publication, created by MadeThought design studio, is enhanced and contained by a bellyband.

Singer stitch
Stitch binding can add a decorative touch as thread is available in many weights and colours, and indeed, can be sewn in a variety of patterns.

Z-binds
This z-bind publication was created by MadeThought design studio. Z-binding clearly separates a publication into two parts.

Elastic bands
Elastic bands provide a simple way of holding loose-leaf sheets together with a rigid cover stock.

Clips and bolts
Clips and bolts and other hardware can be used for binding purposes; as this example by Studio Myerscough design studio shows.

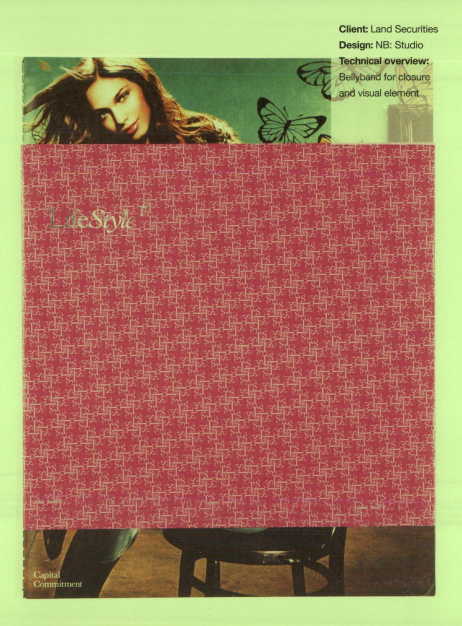

Client: Land Securities
Design: NB: Studio
Technical overview:
Bellyband for closure
and visual element

Perfect binding | **Alternative bindings** | Industry view: Poulin + Morris

Green-coloured stock

K
Y
M
C

Land Securities

This is a brochure called Capital Commitment, which was created by NB: Studio for property development firm Land Securities. The brochure features a printed and foil-blocked bellyband that holds its pages closed in addition to providing a distinctive visual element. The bellyband is marked 'LifeStyle', a slogan that incorporates the client's initials and alludes to the suggestion that the 'right' living space can complement your lifestyle.

Client: The Conran Shop
Design: Studio Myerscough
Technical overview:
Elastic-band binding

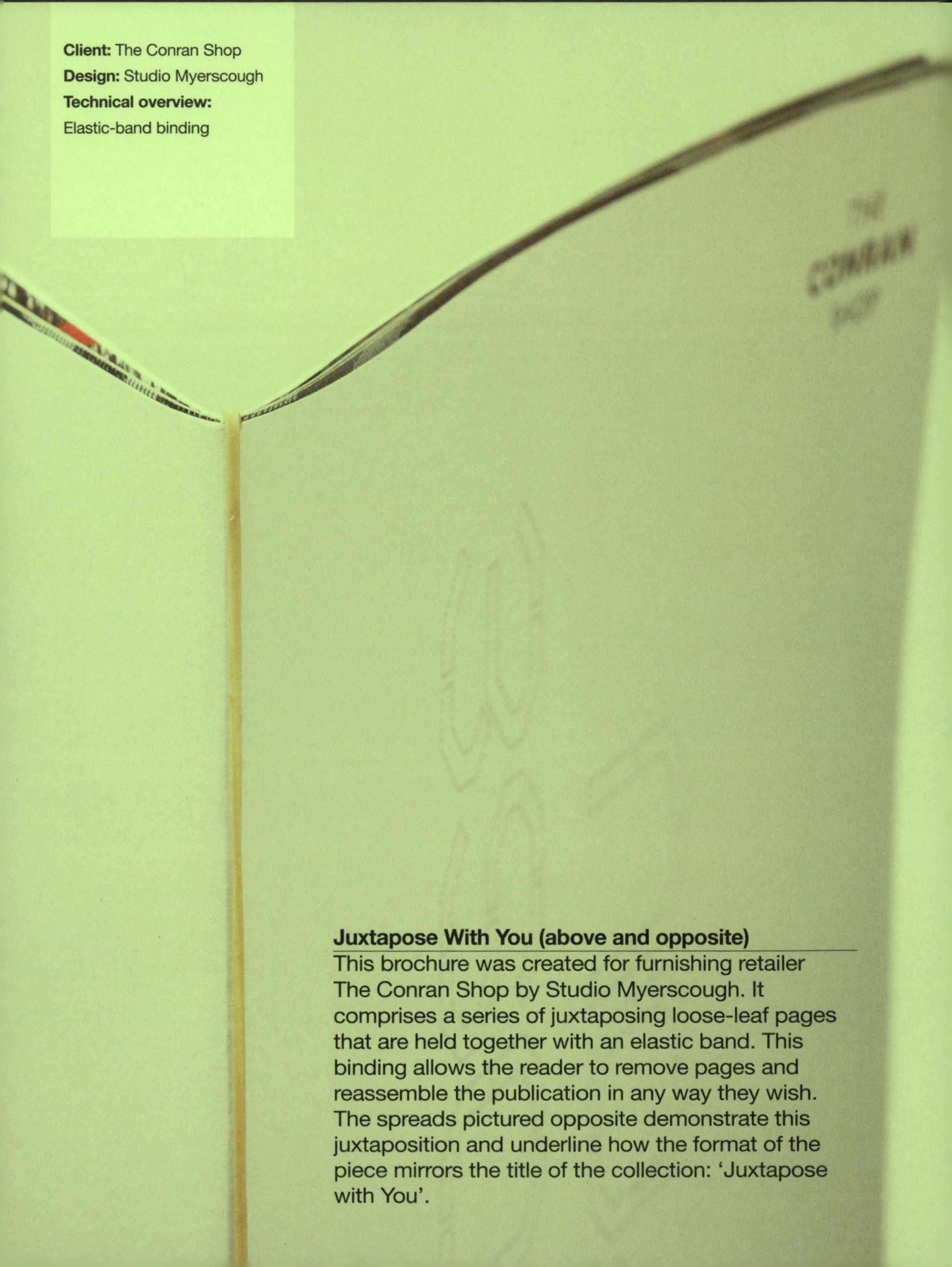

Juxtapose With You (above and opposite)
This brochure was created for furnishing retailer
The Conran Shop by Studio Myerscough. It
comprises a series of juxtaposing loose-leaf pages
that are held together with an elastic band. This
binding allows the reader to remove pages and
reassemble the publication in any way they wish.
The spreads pictured opposite demonstrate this
juxtaposition and underline how the format of the
piece mirrors the title of the collection: 'Juxtapose
with You'.

C M Y K

Industry view: Poulin + Morris

Pictured is *Exposed*, a publication for the School of Visual Arts Senior Library in New York City. This 440-page, full-colour, hardbound volume contains over 100 selections encompassing a wide range of categories: advertising campaigns, book jackets, editorial, graphic identity and branding programmes, packaging, posters, publications, three-dimensional design, and typography.

On a project like this, with so many different printing and finishing techniques, this must rely on a big leap of faith from a client?

That's an understatement! Every year at the School of Visual Arts they produce what is called the Senior Library designed by one of the adjunct professors, of which I am one. It showcases all of the graphic and advertising work of the school and each year there is a different theme, and this particular year it was 'Exposed'. The thematic approach was to allow the work(s) to be shown in a thematic light, and in this case, in a monographic setting - but at the same time use print and finishing techniques to enhance, and indeed explain the work in the book.

That's why we use exposed materials; raw papers, the exposed Smythson binding, using blind finishing as opposed to infilled, such as the blind debossing on binders board. Even down to the outer jacket, an intense fluorescent colour, it is printed on an uncoated, as opposed to a high gloss as you'd normally expect, and this again gives a certain neutrality to the finish.

Poulin + Morris are a New York based multi-disciplinary design studio led by Richard Poulin and Douglas Morris. They have worked across a wide variety of sectors including the arts, communications, finance and healthcare.
www.poulinmorris.com

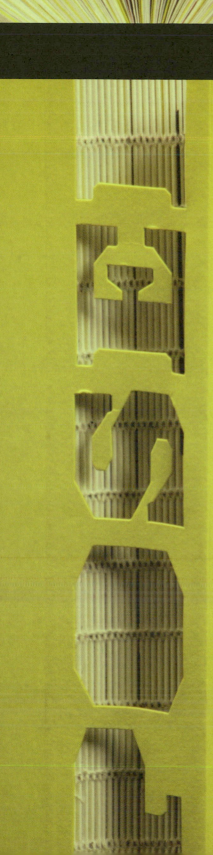

SCHOOL OF VISUAL ARTS

2008 SENIOR LIBRARY

Alternative bindings | **Industry view: Poulin + Morris**

Green-coloured stock

C M Y K

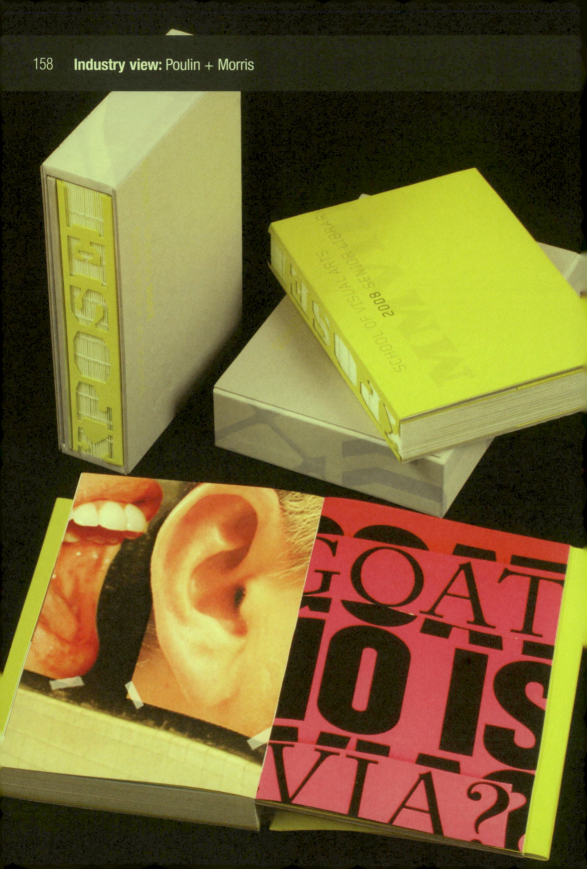

There can be a perception that print and finish techniques are thriftless?

In a project like this there is a very set budget, and the techniques used are only used to tell the story. They are not additions, they are the structure of the story. Apart from the inner text block, that was printed four-colour process on a satin stock, the other materials and processes are what I'd call utilitarian, and the project actually came in under budget. It was my intention with this to create something that allowed the work to be celebrated, so while there are a lot of finishing techniques in here, they are actually very neutral and don't cloud the purpose of the publication.

Alternative bindings | Industry view: Poulin + Morris

Green-coloured stock

C M Y K

Client: The Mill
Design: MadeThought
Grid properties:
Screen-printed jewel box
gives depth and texture

Chapter 6
Resolve

The resolve of a final product often draws together several of the techniques that are discussed in earlier chapters of this book. Many printed items feature a range of creative printing and finishing processes, which ultimately form the final product.

In previous chapters we have looked at the different areas of print and finishing individually. Most pieces of work, however, combine different elements and techniques of both areas. An understanding of the potential of printing and finishing techniques enables a designer to add value to a design through the creative execution of a brief that may result in an enviable finish. This may translate into a direct benefit for the client as their products and communications become more distinctive than their competitors, and ultimately more exciting to the end user.

The satisfaction and interest generated by creative printing and finishing techniques never ceases to astound. People have an instinctive relationship between what they see and what they touch, and the feel of an interesting stock or the way a foil might catch the light possesses a certain magic, one that a designer can control and use to their advantage.

The Mill (opposite)

This packaging for a DVD showreel was created by MadeThought design studio for The Mill, a London-based post-production film company. The jewel box outer has been screen printed on both the front and back to give an element of depth to the design while also adding a textural quality to the product. The screen-printing process gives a flat, even, vibrant colour and with a great deal of fine detail, as can be seen in the grid pattern on the reverse, which lends a unique identity to an otherwise bland, standard packaging item.

Resolve

C M Y K Matt art

Texture

Texture can be given to a publication in several ways; these include substrate choice, printing process and finishing techniques.

Texture adds a tactile quality to a piece of printed matter and, if used effectively, can make for distinctive graphic executions.

Eugène van Veldhoven (above and opposite)

This identity was created by Faydherbe / De Vringer (Wout de Vringer) for fabric designer Eugène van Veldhoven. The design concept reflects the occupation of the client, who creates new coatings and fabrics for the fashion and car industries. Insider, a typeface created by Dutch font studio Character Font Foundry, was used for the text, and the logo was hot-foil blocked and embossed on to a coated metallic paper, which gave it a fabric-like texture. Contact details were printed in a metallic ink and the cards were printed with different varnishes and embosses to create a 'wardrobe' of effects.

Client: Eugène van Veldhoven
Design:
Faydherbe / De Vringer
(Wout de Vringer)
Technical overview:
Foil block and emboss on
to coated metallic paper

Texture | Added value

Matt art

C M Y K

Client: Circle Press
Design: Thomas Manss & Company
Technical overview: Embossed cover and pop-up section add texture

Client: Agenda Vernetta
Design: Lavernia & Cienfuegos
Technical overview:
Embossed pages create a
delicate pattern

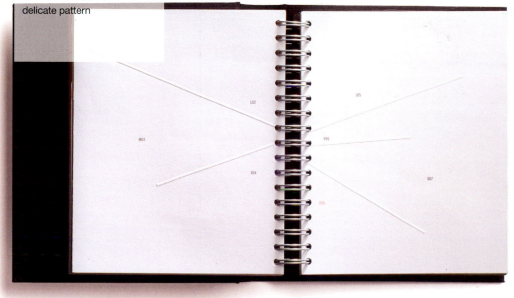

Agenda Vernetta (above)
This diary by Lavernia & Cienfuegos features a delicate series of embossed lines. The tactile effect celebrates the purity in form and design the agency has booome famous for.

The Looking Book (opposite)
The Looking Book was created by Thomas Manss & Company for the 13th anniversary of Circle Press, a company that specializes in publishing unique, imaginative limited-edition books using a range of print processes and finishes. The embossed cover (top), and pop-up section in the centre of the book (bottom right), are original pieces by Circle Press founder and artist Ron King. The other images are taken from Turn Over Darling, a series of six drawings in wire by Ron King.

Texture | Added value

Matt art

K Y M C

CMYK

Client: Fabriano

Design: Thomas Manss & Company

Technical overview: Die-cut book including silk screening and thermography

FABRIANO

COCKTAIL
a night story

10:30 pm

Fabriano Cocktail Visual Book

Thomas Manss & Company created a visual feast with this paper sample book for Fabriano. A rainbow of colours and textures are revealed on the front cover, that mimics the Cocktail moniker. Inside, a series of printing techniques are used including thermography and silk screening, telling a simple story of a cocktail evening.

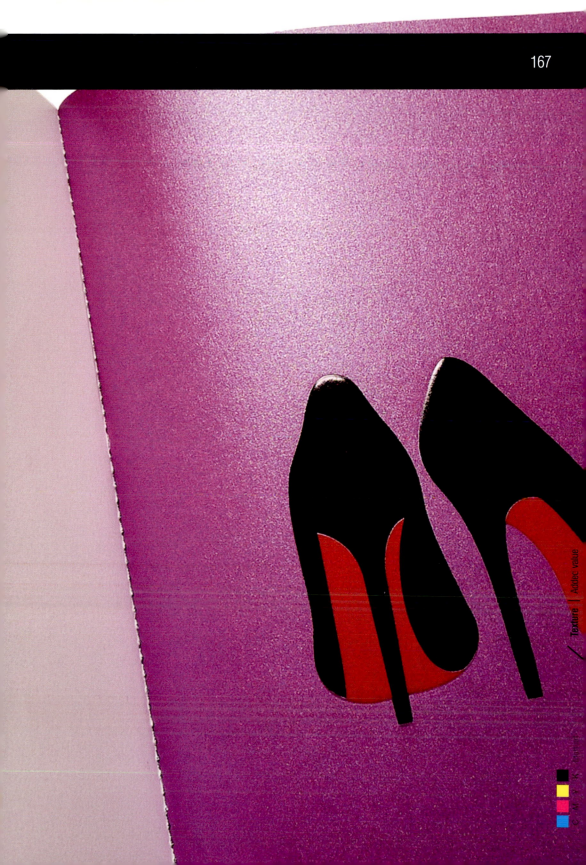

Added value

Printing and finishing techniques provide both the designer and the client with the opportunity to add value to a print publication. While the use of such techniques will undoubtedly add to the cost of a print job they can help the piece communicate effectively and in more dimensions. For example, adding a spot varnish to a cover design will give a publication a tactile element that may translate into a higher perceived quality. The reader may associate this higher quality with the product or organization the publication is from.

Oliver Spencer (opposite)

This brochure was created by George & Vera design studio for a collection of London-based menswear designer Oliver Spencer. The brochure's clean and simple page layout is contained within a four-panel wrap cover to enhance the quality feel of the publication. The brochure is printed on a luxurious uncoated paper stock, and again this alludes to the quality of both the publication and, by association, the clothing line.

Client: Oliver Spencer
Design: George & Vera
Grid properties:
Four-panel wrap cover and
luxurious uncoated stock

Texture | **Added value** | Industry view: Happy F&B

C M Y K   Matt art

Client: VH1

Design: dixonbaxi

Grid properties:
Fore-edge printing and
unusual die cut creates
a designed 'object'

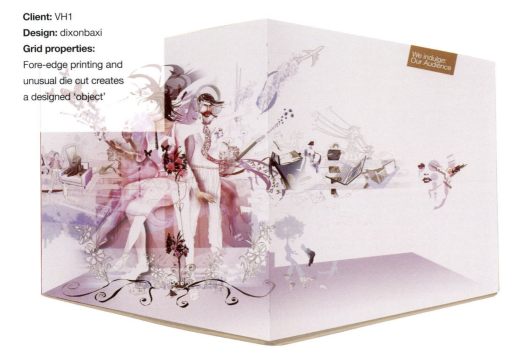

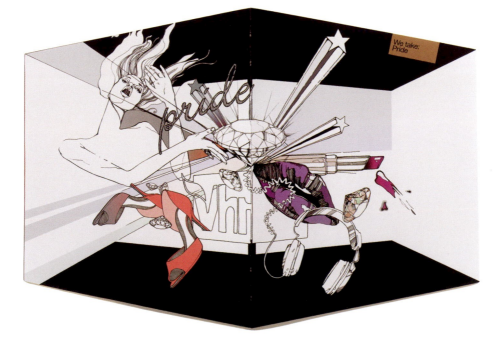

VH1 (below and opposite)

This publication, containing the corporate guidelines for cable TV channel VH1, was created by dixonbaxi design studio. dixonbaxi used the theme of TV idents, which are by nature varied and fleeting, to direct the content. The result is an eclectic array of text and images that is intended to convey a sense that the guidelines are neither prescriptive or restrictive.

The publication has gold fore-edge printing and is die cut in the shape of the channel's logo, creating a designed 'object', rather than just a printed book. The use of fore-edge printing on a publication about an instantaneous medium makes an interesting subversion of the intended longevity the process suggests.

Texture | **Added value** | Industry view: Happy F&B

Matt art

K

Y

M

C

Client: E A Shaw
Design: Simplify
Grid properties:
Outer folder adds value
and importance to the
brochure's contents

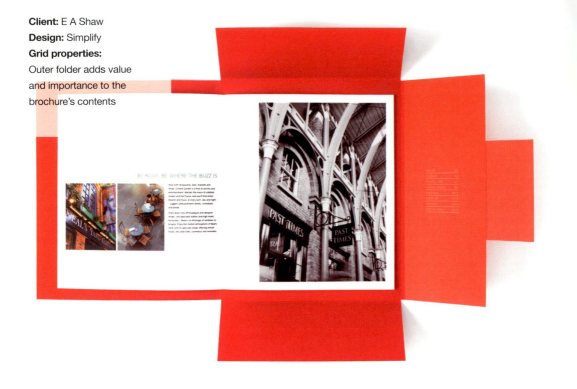

E A Shaw (above)
This promotional brochure for E A Shaw's Ingram House property development in London was created by Simplify design studio. The way the folder contains the inner brochure conveys a sense of value and lends an importance to its contents, in addition to serving as a protective outer. As a property brochure, it will inevitably be well thumbed, so providing extra protection through the outer is a practical idea.

Wedgwood (opposite)
This presentation box, created by Studio Myerscough design studio for fine-china producer Wedgwood, lends a modern touch to a long-standing and traditional brand.

The box is covered with paper and presents a collage design that contains a range of visual elements composed from archival and scanned images and graphic elements, which are combined with an intricate foil pattern. The silver foil maintains the company's classic image as it reflects the ornate moulded designs that embellish Wedgwood's china.

This design concept cleverly revisits traditional values to produce a sense of playful irreverence to an established and historic brand.

Archive Collection

WEDGWOOD
OF BARLASTON

Client: Wedgwood
Design: Studio Myerscough
Grid properties:
Ornate foil design combined with graphics to produce a modern presentation

Texture | **Added value** | Industry view: Happy F&B

C M Y K   Matt art

Industry view: Happy F&B

Pictured are covers from the 2011 edition of the Söderberg Prize – an annual award given to 'an active Nordic designer or craftsman'. The winner, Danish fashion designer Henrik Vibskov adorns the cover.

How do you approach design? This project for instance has a playful nature, and the finishing helps to tell this story.

In all projects, the overall visual solution has to be relevant to the subject. Neither more nor less than it takes to bring out the content. Happy have worked with The Torsten and Wanja Söderberg Prize for more than a decade now, and our aim is always to reflect the prizewinner in some way. To make a tribute to him or her. The design of the catalogue in 2011 was a celebration of the prizewinner, Danish fashion designer Henrik Vibskov. We designed some thirty stickers in various colours, using forms taken from his conceptual world. These were then mounted by hand, in different combinations, on the cover, along with Vibskov's face. The result was 1,200 handmade covers!

Can you elaborate the collaborative relationship between designer, artist and printer?

Collaboration is crucial. But sometimes prestige seems more important than the project itself. At Happy, we stress the necessity of close teamwork on every single job. And not only between our own creatives, but also within our 'extended' team, whether with illustrators, photographers or (not least important) printers. In the latter case, we have a long term relationship with one of Sweden's foremost printers. They have coped with us for a long time now, and always (well, mostly…) support our ideas. They frequently actually refine our ideas, by inventing a new printing method or searching the world for that ideal material. To put it more succinctly, a good idea is dependent on everyone involved in its realization.

Stockholm based Happy F&B, (part of the Forsman & Bodenfors network) work for a wide range of clients, across a range of disciplines including branding, signage and packaging. Their work often challenges conventions, and often has a playful, but powerfully effective resolve.
www.happy.fb.se

Kiss-cut stickers are hand-
applied to to all 1,200 copies of
the book, resulting in eclectic
and individual copies.

Glossary

Printing and finishing processes can be employed to add creative value to a design, as the examples showcased in this volume demonstrate. Understanding the terminology that is used to describe and define these processes enables easier communication of aims and intentions between designers, clients and the print industry.

An appreciation and knowledge of these will facilitate a better understanding and articulation of the subject.

Accordion or concertina fold

Two or more parallel folds that go in opposite directions and open out like an accordion.

Bellyband

A printed band that wraps around the belly of a publication; typically used on magazines.

Bible paper

A thin, lightweight, long-life, opaque paper grade typically made from 25% cotton and linen rags or flax with chemical wood pulp, named after its most common usage.

Binding

Any of several processes for holding together the pages or sections of a publication to form a book, magazine, brochure or some other format using stitches, wire, glue or other media.

Binding screws

Used with the Purdue hard cover binding method to secure a front and back cover to the pages.

Bitmap or raster

Any graphic image that is composed of picture elements (pixels), commonly used to reproduce detailed tonal images.

Bouncer

A registration problem that occurs due to the use of the black process colour. It can be resolved by underprinting the other process colours.

Channel

One layer of colour information in an image. A RGB image has three channels, a CMYK image has four and a black-and-white image has just one.

CMYK

Cyan, magenta, yellow and black, the subtractive primaries and four process colours.

Colour fall

The pages of a publication, as depicted in the imposition plan, which will receive a special colour or varnish, or are to be printed on a different stock.

Concertina fold

See Accordion fold.

Deboss

As emboss, but recessed into the substrate.

Die cut

Special shapes cut in a substrate by a steel die.

Duotone

A tonal image that is produced using two colours.

Duplexing

Lamination of two stocks with different properties such as colour.

Dust jacket

A loose cover to protect the boards of an edition bound book.

Emboss

A design stamped with or without ink or foil into a substrate, giving a raised surface.

Endorse fold

A non-mechanical fold thatcan eliminate the need for binding, thus reducing costs and physical size.

Flock

A speciality stock produced by coating a sheet with size and sprinkling it with a dyed flock powder (made from woollen refuse or vegetable fibre dust), to produce a raised pattern.

Fluorescent colour

A vibrant special colour that cannot be reproduced by combining the process colours.

Foil, heat or hot stamp

Foil pressed on to a substrate using heat and pressure. Also known as block print or foil emboss.

Fore-edge printing
A special printing process for the fore-edge of a publication's pages. Gilding is a form of fore-edge printing.

French fold
A sheet of paper that is only printed on one side and folded with two right-angle folds to form a four-page, uncut section. The section is sewn through the fold while the top edges remain folded and untrimmed.

Gatefold
A type of fold in which the left and right edges fold inwards with parallel folds and meet in the middle of the page without overlapping.

Gradient
A graduation of increasing or decreasing colour(s) applied to an image.

Greyscale
An image that contains shades of grey as well as black and white.

Halftone
The simulation of a continuous tone produced by a pattern of dots.

Imposition
The arrangement of pages in the sequence and position they will appear when printed before being cut, folded and trimmed.

Ink trapping
Overlapping of coloured text or shapes to account for printing misregistration and to prevent the appearance of white gaps.

JPEG (Joint Photographic Experts Group)
A file format for storing photographic images. A JPEG file contains 24-bit colour information (i.e. 6.7 million colours), using compression to discard image information. It is suitable for images with complex pixel gradations but not for flat colour.

Knockout
A gap left in the bottom ink layer so that an overprinted image will appear without colour modification from the ink underneath.

Lacquer
A coating applied to a printed work to provide a high-gloss finish.

Laminate
A stock made by bonding two or more layers together. Typically used to provide a thick cover stock comprising a cheap liner with a printable outer.
Also see Duplexing.

Levels
The amount of colour present within a channel.

Metallic ink
A special printing ink that gives a gold, silver, bronze or copper effect.

Offset lithography
A printing technique in which the ink is transferred from a printing plate to a blanket cylinder and then on to the stock on which it is to be printed. Also called lithography.

Overprint
One element printed over another within a design. Typically, a darker colour will overprint a lighter colour.

Perforation
A series of cuts or holes cut impressed in to a substrate with a die to weaken it for tearing.

Process colours
See CMYK.

Raster
See Bitmap.

Reverse out
The removal of part of a flood colour in order to leave white space.

RGB
Red, green and blue, the additive primary colours.

Screen printing
A low-volume printing method where ink is passed through a screen, which carries a design, on to a substrate.

Silk-screen printing
See Screen printing.

Special colour
A printing ink specially mixed to give a specific colour, including metallic or fluorescent inks.

Spot colour
See Special colour.

Spot varnish
A varnish applied to a specific area of a printed piece.

Stock
The paper to be printed upon.

Substrate
The material or surface to be printed upon.

Surprint
Two elements that are printed on top of one another and are tints of the same colour.

Throw-up
Stock that is folded and bound into a publication in such a way that it can be opened out to a much larger dimension than the publication that contains it.

TIFF (Tagged Image File Format)
A file format for storing halftones and photographic images.

Tint
A colour shade that is predominantly white.

Tip-in
An insert attached to a publication by gluing along the binding edge.

Tonal images
Images produced using black and another colour.

UV coating
Coating applied to a printed substrate that is bonded and cured with ultraviolet light.

Varnish
A clear or tinted liquid shellac or plastic coating put on a printed piece to add a glossy, stain or dull finish, applied like a final ink layer after a piece is printed.

Vellum
A thin sheet of specially prepared calfskin, lambskin, or kidskin leather used as a book-binding material.

Z-bind
A z-shaped cover that is used to join to separate publications, or two parts of the same publication.

Page numbers in *italics* indicate illustrations.

Agency	Contact	Page number
Andrew Hussey	www.andrewhussey.co.uk	100
Aufuldish and Warinner	www.aufwar.com	24, 123
Bedow	www.bedow.se	97
Bruce Mau Design	www.brucemaudesign.com	31
Cartlidge Levene	www.cartlidgelevene.co.uk	45, 149
Creasence	www.creasence.com	7
Dixonbaxi	www.dixonbaxi.com	102, 170, 171
Donnachie, Simionato & Sons (Andy Simionato and Karen ann Donnachie)	www.thisisamagazine.com www.donnachie-simionato.com	126, 127
Frost*	www.frostdesign.co.uk	8, 51, 62, 85, 89, 129
Gabor Palotai	www.gaborpalotai.com	99
George & Vera	www.georgeandvera.com	19, 77, 110, 111, 119, 169
Happy F&B	wwwwww.happy.fb.se	174-177
HGV Felton	www.hgvfelton.com	143
Lavernia Cienfuegos	www.lavernia-cienfuegos.com	165
MadeThought	www.madethought.com	13, 152, 160
Morla Design	www.morladesign.com	131
Morse Studio	www.morsestudio.com	40
NB: Studio	www.nbstudio.co.uk	28, 29, 53, 78, 133, 153
North	www.northdesign.co.uk	80
Parent	www.parentdesign.co.uk	104, 105, 112-115, 132
Poulin Morris	www.poulinmorris.com	95, 156-159
Reform Creative	www.reformcreative.co.uk	107
Rocca Creative	www.roccacreative.co.uk	121
Samuel Muir	www.27london.com	3
SEA Design	www.seadesign.co.uk	18, 34, 35, 36-39, 54-55, 70-71, 103
Simplify	www.fourletterword.co.uk	67, 92, 94, 138, 172
Studio Kluif	www.studiokluif.nl	49
Studio Myerscough	www.studiomyerscough.co.uk	14, 16, 74, 81, 101, 102, 152, 154, 155, 173
Studio Output	www.studio-output.com	98
Studio Thomson	www.studiothomson.co.uk	83
Tank	www.tankmagazine.com	152
Thomas Manss & Company	www.manss.com	12, 17, 20, 33, 59-61, 164
Thirteen	www.thirteen.co.uk	79, 147
Turnbull Grey	www.turnbullgrey.co.uk	11, 15, 47, 66, 91, 93, 96
Turnbull Ripley	www.turnbullripley.co.uk	86, 87
Untitled	www.untitledstudio.com	22, 23, 25, 32, 68, 69, 145, 151
Webb & Webb	www.webbandwebb.co.uk	57
Wout de Vringer	www.woutdevringer.nl	75, 109, 116, 134-137, 162-163